Agnosticism: A Very Short Introduction

VERY SHORT INTRODUCTIONS are for anyone wanting a stimulating and accessible way into a new subject. They are written by experts, and have been translated into more than 45 different languages.

The series began in 1995, and now covers a wide variety of topics in every discipline. The VSI library now contains over 500 volumes—a Very Short Introduction to everything from Psychology and Philosophy of Science to American History and Relativity—and continues to grow in every subject area.

Titles in the series include the following:

AFRICAN HISTORY John Parker and Richard Rathbone
AGEING Nancy A. Pachana
ALGEBRA Peter M. Higgins
AMERICAN HISTORY Paul S. Boyer
AMERICAN IMMIGRATION David A. Gerber
AMERICAN LEGAL HISTORY G. Edward White
AMERICAN POLITICAL HISTORY Donald Critchlow
AMERICAN POLITICAL PARTIES AND ELECTIONS L. Sandy Maisel
AMERICAN POLITICS Richard M. Valelly
THE AMERICAN PRESIDENCY Charles O. Jones
AMERICAN SLAVERY Heather Andrea Williams
ANARCHISM Colin Ward
ANCIENT EGYPT Ian Shaw
ANCIENT GREECE Paul Cartledge
THE ANCIENT NEAR EAST Amanda H. Podany
ANCIENT PHILOSOPHY Julia Annas
ANCIENT WARFARE Harry Sidebottom
ANGLICANISM Mark Chapman
THE ANGLO-SAXON AGE John Blair
ANIMAL BEHAVIOUR Tristram D. Wyatt
ANIMAL RIGHTS David DeGrazia
ANXIETY Daniel Freeman and Jason Freeman
ARCHAEOLOGY Paul Bahn
ARISTOTLE Jonathan Barnes
ART HISTORY Dana Arnold
ART THEORY Cynthia Freeland
ASTROPHYSICS James Binney
ATHEISM Julian Baggini
THE ATMOSPHERE Paul I. Palmer
AUGUSTINE Henry Chadwick
BACTERIA Sebastian G. B. Amyes
BARTHES Jonathan Culler
BEAUTY Roger Scruton
THE BIBLE John Riches
BLACK HOLES Katherine Blundell
BLOOD Chris Cooper
THE BRAIN Michael O'Shea
THE BRICS Andrew F. Cooper
BRITISH POLITICS Anthony Wright
BUDDHA Michael Carrithers
BUDDHISM Damien Keown
BUDDHIST ETHICS Damien Keown
BYZANTIUM Peter Sarris
CANCER Nicholas James
CAPITALISM James Fulcher
CATHOLICISM Gerald O'Collins
THE CELTS Barry Cunliffe
CHEMISTRY Peter Atkins
CHOICE THEORY Michael Allingham
CHRISTIANITY Linda Woodhead
CIRCADIAN RHYTHMS Russell Foster and Leon Kreitzman
CITIZENSHIP Richard Bellamy
CLASSICAL MYTHOLOGY Helen Morales
CLASSICS Mary Beard and John Henderson

CLIMATE Mark Maslin
CLIMATE CHANGE Mark Maslin
THE COLD WAR Robert McMahon
COMBINATORICS Robin Wilson
COMMUNISM Leslie Holmes
COMPUTER SCIENCE Subrata Dasgupta
CONSCIOUSNESS Susan Blackmore
CONTEMPORARY ART
    Julian Stallabrass
CORAL REEFS Charles Sheppard
COSMOLOGY Peter Coles
THE CRUSADES Christopher Tyerman
DADA AND SURREALISM
    David Hopkins
DANTE Peter Hainsworth and
    David Robey
DARWIN Jonathan Howard
THE DEAD SEA SCROLLS
    Timothy Lim
DECOLONIZATION Dane Kennedy
DEMOCRACY Bernard Crick
DESIGN John Heskett
DINOSAURS David Norman
DREAMING J. Allan Hobson
DRUGS Les Iversen
DRUIDS Barry Cunliffe
THE EARTH Martin Redfern
ECONOMICS Partha Dasgupta
EGYPTIAN MYTH Geraldine Pinch
THE ELEMENTS Philip Ball
EMOTION Dylan Evans
EMPIRE Stephen Howe
ENGLISH LITERATURE Jonathan Bate
THE ENLIGHTENMENT
    John Robertson
EPICUREANISM Catherine Wilson
EPIDEMIOLOGY Rodolfo Saracci
ETHICS Simon Blackburn
EUGENICS Philippa Levine
THE EUROPEAN UNION John Pinder
    and Simon Usherwood
EVOLUTION Brian and
    Deborah Charlesworth
EXISTENTIALISM Thomas Flynn
FASCISM Kevin Passmore
FEMINISM Margaret Walters
THE FIRST WORLD WAR
    Michael Howard
FORENSIC PSYCHOLOGY
    David Canter

FOUCAULT Gary Gutting
FREE SPEECH Nigel Warburton
FREE WILL Thomas Pink
FREUD Anthony Storr
FUNDAMENTALISM Malise Ruthven
FUNGI Nicholas P. Money
GALAXIES John Gribbin
GALILEO Stillman Drake
GAME THEORY Ken Binmore
GANDHI Bhikhu Parekh
GEOGRAPHY John Matthews and
    David Herbert
GEOPOLITICS Klaus Dodds
GLOBAL CATASTROPHES Bill McGuire
GLOBAL ECONOMIC HISTORY
    Robert C. Allen
GLOBALIZATION Manfred Steger
GOD John Bowker
HABERMAS James Gordon Finlayson
HEGEL Peter Singer
HINDUISM Kim Knott
HISTORY John H. Arnold
THE HISTORY OF LIFE Michael Benton
THE HISTORY OF MATHEMATICS
    Jacqueline Stedall
THE HISTORY OF MEDICINE
    William Bynum
THE HISTORY OF TIME
    Leofranc Holford-Strevens
HIV AND AIDS Alan Whiteside
HOLLYWOOD Peter Decherney
HUMAN ANATOMY
    Leslie Klenerman
HUMAN EVOLUTION Bernard Wood
HUMAN RIGHTS Andrew Clapham
IDEOLOGY Michael Freeden
INDIAN PHILOSOPHY Sue Hamilton
INFINITY Ian Stewart
INFORMATION Luciano Floridi
INNOVATION Mark Dodgson and
    David Gann
INTELLIGENCE Ian J. Deary
INTERNATIONAL
    MIGRATION Khalid Koser
INTERNATIONAL RELATIONS
    Paul Wilkinson
ISLAM Malise Ruthven
ISLAMIC HISTORY Adam Silverstein
JESUS Richard Bauckham
JOURNALISM Ian Hargreaves

JUDAISM Norman Solomon
JUNG Anthony Stevens
KABBALAH Joseph Dan
KANT Roger Scruton
KNOWLEDGE Jennifer Nagel
THE KORAN Michael Cook
LATE ANTIQUITY Gillian Clark
LAW Raymond Wacks
THE LAWS OF THERMODYNAMICS
    Peter Atkins
LEADERSHIP Keith Grint
LEARNING Mark Haselgrove
LIGHT Ian Walmsley
LINGUISTICS Peter Matthews
LITERARY THEORY Jonathan Culler
LOCKE John Dunn
LOGIC Graham Priest
MACHIAVELLI Quentin Skinner
MARTIN LUTHER Scott H. Hendrix
MARTYRDOM Jolyon Mitchell
MARX Peter Singer
MATHEMATICS Timothy Gowers
THE MEANING OF LIFE Terry Eagleton
MEASUREMENT David Hand
MEDICAL ETHICS Tony Hope
MEDIEVAL BRITAIN John Gillingham
    and Ralph A. Griffiths
MEDIEVAL LITERATURE
    Elaine Treharne
MEDIEVAL PHILOSOPHY
    John Marenbon
MEMORY Jonathan K. Foster
METAPHYSICS Stephen Mumford
MICROSCOPY Terence Allen
MILITARY JUSTICE Eugene R. Fidell
MODERN ART David Cottington
MODERN CHINA Rana Mitter
MODERN IRELAND Senia Pašeta
MODERN ITALY Anna Cento Bull
MODERN JAPAN
    Christopher Goto-Jones
MODERNISM Christopher Butler
MOLECULAR BIOLOGY Aysha Divan
    and Janice A. Royds
MOLECULES Philip Ball
MOONS David A. Rothery
MUSIC Nicholas Cook
MYTH Robert A. Segal
NEOLIBERALISM Manfred Steger and
    Ravi Roy

NEWTON Robert Iliffe
NIETZSCHE Michael Tanner
NORTH AMERICAN INDIANS
    Theda Perdue and Michael D. Green
NORTHERN IRELAND
    Marc Mulholland
NOTHING Frank Close
NUCLEAR PHYSICS Frank Close
NUTRITION David A. Bender
THE PALESTINIAN-ISRAELI
    CONFLICT Martin Bunton
PANDEMICS Christian W. McMillen
PARTICLE PHYSICS Frank Close
THE PERIODIC TABLE Eric R. Scerri
PHILOSOPHY Edward Craig
PHILOSOPHY IN THE ISLAMIC
    WORLD Peter Adamson
PHILOSOPHY OF LAW
    Raymond Wacks
PHILOSOPHY OF SCIENCE
    Samir Okasha
PHOTOGRAPHY Steve Edwards
PHYSICAL CHEMISTRY Peter Atkins
PLANETS David A. Rothery
PLATO Julia Annas
POLITICAL PHILOSOPHY David Miller
POLITICS Kenneth Minogue
POPULISM Cas Mudde and
    Cristóbal Rovira Kaltwasser
POSTCOLONIALISM Robert Young
POSTMODERNISM Christopher Butler
POSTSTRUCTURALISM
    Catherine Belsey
PREHISTORY Chris Gosden
PRESOCRATIC PHILOSOPHY
    Catherine Osborne
PSYCHIATRY Tom Burns
PSYCHOLOGY Gillian Butler and
    Freda McManus
PSYCHOTHERAPY Tom Burns and
    Eva Burns-Lundgren
PUBLIC HEALTH Virginia Berridge
QUANTUM THEORY
    John Polkinghorne
RACISM Ali Rattansi
THE REFORMATION Peter Marshall
RELATIVITY Russell Stannard
THE RENAISSANCE Jerry Brotton
RENAISSANCE ART
    Geraldine A. Johnson

REVOLUTIONS Jack A. Goldstone
RHETORIC Richard Toye
RISK Baruch Fischhoff and John Kadvany
RITUAL Barry Stephenson
RIVERS Nick Middleton
ROBOTICS Alan Winfield
ROMAN BRITAIN Peter Salway
THE ROMAN EMPIRE
    Christopher Kelly
THE ROMAN REPUBLIC
    David M. Gwynn
RUSSIAN HISTORY Geoffrey Hosking
THE RUSSIAN REVOLUTION
    S. A. Smith
SCHIZOPHRENIA Chris Frith and
    Eve Johnstone
SCIENCE AND RELIGION
    Thomas Dixon
SEXUALITY Véronique Mottier
SHAKESPEARE'S COMEDIES
    Bart van Es
SIKHISM Eleanor Nesbitt
SLEEP Steven W. Lockley and
    Russell G. Foster
SOCIAL AND CULTURAL
    ANTHROPOLOGY
    John Monaghan and Peter Just
SOCIAL PSYCHOLOGY Richard J. Crisp
SOCIAL WORK Sally Holland and
    Jonathan Scourfield
SOCIALISM Michael Newman
SOCIOLOGY Steve Bruce

SOCRATES C. C. W. Taylor
SOUND Mike Goldsmith
THE SOVIET UNION Stephen Lovell
THE SPANISH CIVIL WAR
    Helen Graham
SPANISH LITERATURE Jo Labanyi
STATISTICS David J. Hand
STUART BRITAIN John Morrill
SYMMETRY Ian Stewart
TAXATION Stephen Smith
TELESCOPES Geoff Cottrell
TERRORISM Charles Townshend
THEOLOGY David F. Ford
TIBETAN BUDDHISM
    Matthew T. Kapstein
THE TROJAN WAR Eric H. Cline
THE TUDORS John Guy
THE UNITED NATIONS
    Jussi M. Hanhimäki
THE U.S. CONGRESS Donald A. Ritchie
THE U.S. SUPREME COURT
    Linda Greenhouse
THE VIKINGS Julian Richards
VIRUSES Dorothy H. Crawford
WAR AND TECHNOLOGY
    Alex Roland
WILLIAM SHAKESPEARE
    Stanley Wells
WITCHCRAFT Malcolm Gaskill
THE WORLD TRADE
    ORGANIZATION Amrita Narlikar
WORLD WAR II Gerhard L. Weinberg

Robin Le Poidevin

AGNOSTICISM

A Very Short Introduction

OXFORD
UNIVERSITY PRESS

OXFORD

UNIVERSITY PRESS

Great Clarendon Street, Oxford OX2 6DP

Oxford University Press is a department of the University of Oxford.
It furthers the University's objective of excellence in research, scholarship,
and education by publishing worldwide in

Oxford New York

Auckland Cape Town Dar es Salaam Hong Kong Karachi
Kuala Lumpur Madrid Melbourne Mexico City Nairobi
New Delhi Shanghai Taipei Toronto

With offices in

Argentina Austria Brazil Chile Czech Republic France Greece
Guatemala Hungary Italy Japan Poland Portugal Singapore
South Korea Switzerland Thailand Turkey Ukraine Vietnam

Oxford is a registered trade mark of Oxford University Press
in the UK and in certain other countries

Published in the United States
by Oxford University Press Inc., New York

British Library Cataloguing in Publication Data

Data available

Library of Congress Cataloging in Publication Data

Data available

Typeset by SPI Publisher Services, Pondicherry, India
Printed in Great Britain by
Ashford Colour Press Ltd, Gosport, Hampshire

ISBN: 978–0–19–957526–8

5 7 9 10 8 6

For Hatty

Contents

Preface xiii

List of illustrations xv

Introduction 1

1 What is agnosticism? 8

2 Who were the first agnostics? 18

3 Is agnosticism necessary? 40

4 Why be agnostic? 54

5 Does agnosticism rest on a mistake? 77

6 How should the agnostic live? 97

7 How should agnosticism be taught? 108

References 119

Further reading 123

Index 131

Preface

Many different kinds of book could be written about agnosticism. It is a topic that invites exploration from a variety of angles. It might, for instance, be the focus of a sociological survey of contemporary religious attitudes. Or it might be one aspect of an examination of negative theology, a feature of a number of religious traditions in which God's nature is presented as largely or wholly unknown and unknowable. Yet again, it might be part of a history of leading Victorian intellectuals. This little volume, however, is none of these. Although there is some history in it, for which I am much indebted to Bernard Lightman's illuminating book *The Origins of Agnosticism*, what I present here views agnosticism from a philosophical angle. The key question is whether or not agnosticism is justified, whether or not it is the right attitude to take towards that most urgent of issues, the existence of God. It is an invitation to the reader to engage in debate, and that involves a certain amount of to-ing and fro-ing between different positions. It is a feature of philosophical writing that positions are often presented, only then to be criticized and opposed, and that can be a little disconcerting to readers not already familiar with this style: just what position, they may wonder, is the author taking? So, in case there is any doubt, what is offered here is a defence of agnosticism, of a fairly strong kind. But, and this may seem surprising, it is an agnosticism that (I argue) is compatible with a religious way of life and outlook.

had to be very selective about the individuals I discuss. seem odd, for example, that there is no mention of the escribed as 'The Great Agnostic', Robert G. Ingersoll (1833–99), an American lawyer who became famous as an orator, giving hugely popular talks on a variety of topics, often with a humanist theme. But Ingersoll's mission was not to promote agnosticism so much as emancipation from religion. Asked whether he thought agnosticism was superior to atheism, he replied that there was no difference between them. That is not the line I wish to take here.

I would like to thank all those who have helped this project on its way: Andrea Keegan, who commissioned the book, and offered advice and encouragement in the early stages, Emma Marchant, who saw it through to completion, Carrie Hickman, who provided the illustrations, and two readers for the Press who offered detailed comments on the draft typescript.

RLeP, April 2010

List of Illustrations

1 Cover of *The Agnostic Annual*,
   1897 **3**
   The Bodleian Library, University of
   Oxford (Per. 13005 d.9/1897, T/Pages)

2 Sextus Empiricus **12**
   The Granger Collection/TopFoto

3 Thomas Henry Huxley **20**
   The Granger Collection/TopFoto

4 Henry Longueville Mansel **24**
   © National Portrait Gallery, London

5 Immanuel Kant **28**
   The Granger Collection/TopFoto

6 David Hume **32**
   TopFoto/Fotomas

7 The celestial teapot **43**
   © Artwork by Sam Meakin

8 A. J. Ayer **80**
   © 2006 John Hedgecoe/Topfoto

9 William Kingdom Clifford **92**
   © National Portrait Gallery, London

10 William James **95**
    © Antman Archives/The Image
    Works/TopFoto

11 Richard Dawkins **110**
    Jon Worth/British Humanist
    Association

Introduction

One of the first privileges granted to Adam is that of naming all the animals in the Garden of Eden:

> And out of the ground the LORD God formed every beast of the field, and every fowl of the air; and brought them unto Adam to see what he would call them: and whatsoever Adam called every living creature, that was the name thereof.

It is symbolic of his dominion over the other inhabitants of the garden, but it also gives him the power to talk and think about them, not simply as individuals, but as naturally divided groups. Naming is important. A name provides a focus for thought and feeling. In commercial and political life, this process of naming is called 'branding'. An immense amount of thought goes into the branding of a new product, a new company, a new political party. So important is it, indeed, that it is sometimes thought necessary to *rebrand* something that isn't new at all, but needs to be presented to the public in a new way. No doubt something is different: a new ingredient, a new shape, a new orientation, a new ideological focus, a new generation of dynamic young leaders, and so on. But often, just the coining of a name itself has the power to change attitudes.

As an attitude, agnosticism is very old indeed, probably as old as the first speculations about the nature of the cosmos and our place and purpose within it. But as a name, 'agnosticism' has been around for fewer than 150 years. This particular branding had every effect that could have been desired: it became a focus of interest, of debate. Alliances formed around it. It even led to a new periodical: *The Agnostic Annual*. And it is now a staple of religious education in schools: pupils are taught that there is theism, there is atheism, and there is agnosticism.

Unfortunately, branding can backfire. The evoked feelings may be hostile. Agnosticism has certainly had a bad press, and continues to do so. The people who first called themselves agnostics were viewed with great suspicion. They were, it was suggested, just atheists under a different name. In more recent times, agnostics have been derided for indecisiveness. Look, for instance, at the attitudes Richard Dawkins reports in *The God Delusion*:

> The robust Muscular Christian haranguing us from the pulpit of my old school chapel admitted a sneaking regard for atheists. They at least had the courage of their misguided convictions. What this preacher couldn't stand was agnostics: namby-pamby, mushy pap, weak tea, weedy, pallid fence-sitters … In the same vein, according to Quentin de la Bédoyère, the Catholic historian Hugh Ross Williamson 'respected the committed religious believer and also the committed atheist. He reserved his contempt for the wishy-washy boneless mediocrities who flapped around in the middle.'

Dawkins himself is a biologist, committed atheist, and highly effective communicator of science and its apparently anti-religious implications. Since this passage occurs at the beginning of a section entitled 'The Poverty of Agnosticism', it is evident that Dawkins is somewhat sympathetic to such attitudes. As we shall see, however, his own response is more measured.

So what is agnosticism, that it should provoke such opprobrium? A common view is that it is nothing more than ticking the 'don't know' box on the question of God's existence. If that is all it is,

THE LITERARY GUIDE: A Rationalist Review. Monthly, 2d.

THE

AGNOSTIC

ANNUAL

~ 1897. ~

EDITED BY CHARLES A. WATTS.

From Rome to Rationalism ; or, Why I Left the Church
                JOSEPH McCABE (*lately* FATHER ANTONY, F.S.O.)
Theology in State Schools : The Latest Organised Hypocrisy
                            J. ALLANSON PICTON
Larrendill : A Poem . . . . W. STEWART ROSS (SALADIN)
Agnosticism in Allegory . . . . . . AMOS WATERS
An Address to Orthodox Christians . . . . CHARLES WATTS
Hindrances to Rationalist Propaganda . R. BITHELL, B.Sc., Ph.D.
Immortality : A Poem . . . . . GEORGE ANDERSON
The Progress of Religious Thought . . . . JULIAN
At the House of Chloe . . . . . F. J. GOULD
Immortality as the Object of Life . . CHARLES T. GORHAM

LONDON :
WATTS & CO., 17, JOHNSON'S COURT, FLEET STREET, E.C.
Price Sixpence.

WHY LIVE A MORAL LIFE ?—*A Symposium.* 6d. (WATTS & CO.)

TALES FROM THE BIBLE TOLD TO MY DAUGHTER. IN (WATTS & CO.)

A CONCISE HISTORY OF RELIGION. Vol. I., 2s. 6d. ; Vol. II., 3s. 6d. (WATTS & CO.)

Introduction

1. Victorian branding: cover page of the 1897 issue of *The Agnostic Annual*

then it isn't surprising that it does not always command the respect of those with more decided opinions. Also common is the view that it is some kind of compromise between theism and atheism – between belief that God does exist and belief that he doesn't – a view that tries to please both sides of the debate and, like most compromises, ends up pleasing neither. It stands, it seems, for lack of belief or commitment, for indecision, for non-engagement.

If this is all agnosticism is, why devote a book to it, even one as short as this? It is as if someone wrote a book entitled *My Theory of the Universe* and announced on the first page that he didn't have one. What would the rest of the book contain? And in this series of *Very Short Introductions*, a volume on agnosticism seems something of an odd one out. The other volumes are on positive themes: beliefs that have defined a culture, events that have shaped nations, ideas and discoveries that have transformed human thought and existence. In contrast, agnosticism seems relentlessly negative, a non-idea, an absence. It doesn't provoke action so much as inhibit it, since indecision leads to inactivity. If it is worth writing about at all, it is simply as a social phenomenon, a factor in the decline of religion.

Or so its detractors would have us believe. To see what kind of subject there might be, if any, for further study, let us take a quick preliminary look at the fairness of these common attitudes towards agnosticism.

Is agnosticism just an acknowledgement that one doesn't know? No doubt many people who describe themselves as agnostics mean this and no more. But the first people to call themselves agnostics meant something more, something that involved an appeal to *principle*. That involved reflection on the nature of knowledge itself, and the ways in which we acquire it. Agnosticism was for them the result of intellectual struggle, not an unwillingness to engage with that struggle.

Consider next the idea that agnosticism represents a failure of nerve, a refuge for the intellectually and morally infirm, for 'weedy, pallid fence-sitters'. It's odd that prolonged fence-sitting should be thought to be an occupation for the constitutionally delicate: it is in fact an extremely uncomfortable position to hold for any length of time. Instead of a resting place, why should it not be a spur to action, a recognition of the need for further inquiry? And if, as in the case of the 19th-century agnostics, it is the result of sustained thought, and means going against the current of socially acceptable attitudes, that requires both honesty and courage.

But this picture of agnosticism as the result of careful thought, rather than a failure to think, leads to a further criticism, that agnostics are simply not reasonable. Their affecting not to know, if based on principle, must be based on far too stringent a criterion for knowledge. They must be looking for absolute certainty, and such certainty is not to be had, on almost any matter. So if we are obliged to be agnostic about God, then we should be agnostic about fairies, ghosts, elves, the Man in the Moon, magic, astrological influence, the Loch Ness Monster etc. Like a virus, agnosticism is liable to spread. Lack of commitment in one sphere will infect other beliefs, and we will find ourselves embracing agnosticism about the existence of small pixies that make the grass grow during the night. But most of us are not agnostic about such things, nor should we be. Even if we cannot prove them, we think that we have good grounds for many of our beliefs, and that is enough, in most cases, for us to claim knowledge. So, to be taken seriously, agnostics need to show that they are not setting the standards for knowledge too high, and that their reasons for disavowing knowledge in one case will not apply equally to others.

Even its critics concede that, in some circumstances and on some subjects, agnosticism is reasonable. As Dawkins points out, 'there is nothing wrong with being agnostic in cases where we lack evidence one way or the other. It is the reasonable position.' It is currently reasonable to be agnostic about the existence of extra-terrestrial life, for instance. This reminds us that agnosticism as a phenomenon is not confined to the religious domain. There is what we might call scientific agnosticism, a suspension of belief, or commitment, concerning the subject matter of science. And, when it is focused on particular phenomena and theories, it is a proper part of the scientific attitude. It is also an appropriate response to the breakdown of previously solid and seemingly invulnerable structures of thought. When in 1973 the Harvard economist J. K. Galbraith was invited by the BBC to present a television series on economic history, he chose the title *The Age of Uncertainty*, the idea being to

> contrast the great certainties in economic thought in the last century with the great uncertainty with which problems are faced in our time. In the last century capitalists were certain of the success of capitalism, socialists of socialism, imperialists of colonialism, and the ruling classes knew that they were meant to rule. Little of this certainty now survives. Given the dismaying complexity of the problems mankind now faces, it would surely be odd if it did.

The uncertainty has not diminished since 1973. Indeed, in the global economic crisis that characterizes the time of writing (2009), it has, if anything, increased. Political and economic upheavals – revolution, war, inflation, depression, collapse of the stock market – have all contributed to this uncertainty. Similarly, agnosticism about religious belief in the 19th century took place in the context of intellectual upheavals: new methods of biblical criticism, Darwin's theory of the origin of species, and philosophical attacks on 'metaphysics'.

We might characterize agnosticism as that state of mind in which we realize that doubts about once unquestioned beliefs are not going to go away, to be replaced either by a confident reaffirmation of those beliefs or else an equally confident rejection of them.

Dawkins argues, however, that in those cases where theories are capable of being tested, the reasonable kind of agnosticism is a purely temporary position, a provisional suspension of belief while we wait for the evidence to arrive. Once it does, neutrality is no longer defensible. Agnosticism about the existence of a benevolent creator, who made man in his own image, and allowed living things to prosper on the Earth, may have been reasonable in the middle of the 19th century. But now we understand the processes of the evolution of species, the adaptation of organisms to their environment, the survival of the fittest, and so on, it is reasonable no longer. Atheism is now the most reasonable stance. Religious agnosticism may have been prompted by legitimate challenges to belief, but what sustains it is an unreasonable demand for absolute proof when the evidence is staring us in the face. That is a challenge to which the agnostic must respond.

This brief consideration of anti-agnostic attitudes leaves us with plenty of questions. In the pages that follow, I try to address some of them. First, we consider what agnosticism really is: is it a belief, or the absence of belief? Then we take a look at its history. Who were the first people to call themselves agnostics? To what extent were their views anticipated in earlier thought? Next, we ask whether we really need agnosticism. If we can't establish God's existence, shouldn't there be a presumption of atheism? We then examine the case for agnosticism. Are there positive arguments in favour of it? Next, we ask whether agnosticism is based on a mistake. Once we are clear about the true nature of such things as religious faith, moral attitudes, and scientific theory, doesn't agnosticism turn out to be founded on a false conception of such things? We then consider more practical matters. How should agnostics live their agnosticism? Could it make sense to live a religious life while being wholly agnostic about the truth of religious belief? Finally, we turn to education. How should agnosticism be taught? Should schools teach religions from an explicitly agnostic perspective?

There is no shortage of controversy here. Agnostics have a case to answer – but so do their opponents.

Chapter 1
What is agnosticism?

Caught in the middle?

Where does agnosticism sit in the spectrum of beliefs about God? Let's start with the two views mentioned earlier: that agnosticism is the 'don't know' position on God's existence, and that it is a compromise between theism and atheism, a 'flapping around' in the middle.

These two views of it aren't entirely compatible. If agnosticism just stands for a 'don't know' position, then it is hardly in the middle between theism and atheism. A middle position would be an answer to the same question that theists and atheists are answering. It is the question 'Does God exist?' The theist says 'yes' and the atheist 'no'. But 'don't know' is not an *answer* to this question. It is certainly a *response* to it, a response that is acceptable in a way in which 'the wardrobe' is not. But it is not an answer. Rather, it is an admission that one doesn't have an answer. It is a comment on, or attitude towards, the debate between theists and atheists, not a position within that debate. The question many theists, atheists, and agnostics are prepared to answer is whether we can establish that God does or does not exist. But even here, the agnostics are not to be found in the middle. They will be on the opposite side from those theists and atheists who think that one can establish whether or not God exists. And not all atheists and theists do affirm this. It is possible to be an agnostic atheist, one who does not believe in God, and does not permit the idea to have any practical impact on their life, while acknowledging that they do not have substantial grounds for disbelief. And there most certainly are agnostic theists. Indeed, every major religion exhibits a substantial element of agnosticism somewhere within its traditional system of thought. One that did not would be dangerous indeed.

Suppose, however, that we were to represent attitudes towards God on a sliding scale, ranging from absolute confidence that he exists to absolute confidence that he doesn't. Most of us will be somewhere between those extremes. And it seems reasonable to label the area around the middle of this scale 'agnosticism', allowing it to shade gradually (with no determinate cut-off points) into theism in one direction and atheism in the other. But the problem with this kind of sliding scale is that it is one-dimensional. It ignores important distinctions that help to bring out some of the subtleties of debate over agnosticism. Let us take a look at them.

'Weak' versus 'strong'

The first distinction we will need to make is between two strengths of agnosticism. 'Weak agnosticism' is the position most people are familiar with, and is nothing more than a confession that one does not know whether God exists. This is the position we can locate roughly in the middle of the sliding scale just mentioned. Weak agnosticism by itself is just a personal matter: it makes no comment on others' beliefs.

Strong agnosticism is more interesting. It says that we *cannot* know whether or not God exists. There is something about the subject matter that makes knowledge impossible in this case. That, of course, has to be based on some criterion by which we can judge what counts as knowledge. The more stringent the criterion, the more secure, but also the less interesting, the resulting agnosticism. The most interesting, and boldest, agnosticism says that we cannot even have justified beliefs in this area.

The adjectives 'weak' and 'strong' are not meant to imply anything about the mental capacities or moral character of those who adopt these positions: it is simply an indication of the logical relationship between the two ideas. Strong agnosticism is the 'stronger' of the two just in the sense that it implies weak agnosticism, whereas weak agnosticism does not imply strong agnosticism. If your criterion for knowledge tells you that you cannot make knowledge claims where God is concerned (strong agnosticism) then, in consistency, you will admit that you do not know whether God exists (weak agnosticism). The converse does not hold. Admitting that one doesn't know does not necessarily indicate some background principle concerning what knowledge amounts to. Lack of knowledge can be the result of any number of factors: you may not have considered the matter much, or you have but find the evidence ambiguous, or reasons to doubt have occurred to you, and so on.

Strong agnosticism might determine your position on the sliding scale of certainties, but it is not itself a position on that scale.

'Local' versus 'global'

Agnosticism is always agnosticism *about* something. It may be about God, or it may be about alien life, or the possibility of a Grand Unified Theory of physics, or the wisdom of taking vitamin pills, and so on. And even when it has to do with God, it needn't specifically be to do with his existence. Those who are prepared to commit to God's existence may be agnostic about certain or even all of God's properties. It is an entirely orthodox view in theistic religions that human language is inadequate to capture God. This view was often expressed by medieval theologians. St Anselm (1033–1109), an Italian philosopher who became Archbishop of

Canterbury, famously defined God as 'that than which no greater can be conceived'. It follows from this definition, not that God is the greatest being imaginable, but, Anselm explains, something that transcends our thought:

> Therefore, Lord, not only are You that than which a greater cannot be thought, but You are also something greater than can be thought. For since it is possible to think that there is such a one, then, if You are not this same being something greater than You could be thought – which cannot be.

According to 'negative theology', or the *via negativa* (the negative way), we can say what God is *not* like, but can only gesture (and perhaps not even that) at what he is like. His essential nature remains unknown. The Jewish philosopher Moses Maimonides (1135–1204) was one of the most prominent proponents of this view.

The Italian philosopher and theologian St Thomas Aquinas (1224–74), considering the question whether it is possible for anyone in this life to see God's essence, to see him as he really is, concludes:

> A mere man cannot see the essence of God unless he be lifted out of this mortal life. The reason for this is that...the way in which a thing knows depends on the way it has its being. Our souls, so long as we are in this life, have their being in corporeal matter; hence they cannot by nature know anything except what has its form in matter or what can be known through such a form. It is obvious, however, that the divine essence cannot be known through the nature of material things...

Theistic religion naturally engenders this kind of agnosticism precisely because it draws attention to the fact that God's greatness so far surpasses our own, and that our own understanding is infinitely feeble in comparison with his. Theism

SEXTUS EMPYRICUS

Ex numismate æreo.

2. Sextus Empiricus, preserver and recorder of Pyrrhonian
scepticism, the ancient world's most wide-ranging and devastating
attack on human knowledge

thus cultivates a degree of mystery. (This is not intended as criticism, just a neutral statement of fact.)

Most agnosticism, then, is *local*: it is applied to a particular subject matter. An agnostic about aliens need not be agnostic about God. And within any given subject matter, one might be agnostic only about certain aspects. A biologist deeply committed to the truth of genetic mutation may nevertheless be agnostic (though perhaps only provisionally so) about the precise mechanism underlying that mutation. A Christian believer may still be agnostic about how God answers prayers, why he permits evil, how he became incarnate in Christ – or even whether he did. For most of this book, the focus is on agnosticism with respect to the existence, rather than the nature, of God: a form of local agnosticism.

A totally *global* agnosticism is not confined to a particular subject matter. One could, perhaps, imagine someone who was completely agnostic about everything. Have there been any such global agnostics? Perhaps the closest we can find would be the Pyrrhonian sceptics of the 1st century BC (see Chapter 2), who came up with a large number of sophisticated arguments designed to unsettle confidence in our capacity to gain knowledge about the world. They drew attention not only to the unreliability of the senses, but also to the contradictory nature of the most common-sensical of beliefs, undermining even reason itself. In practice, of course, we can't suspend all our beliefs, since our actions are determined by those beliefs and a completely passive existence would be impossible to sustain. Global agnosticism, it seems, would not be a serious option.

Evidential agnosticism

It is some time during the 1960s and a group of cosmologists is considering two rival hypotheses about the origins of the universe. One hypothesis – the 'Steady State' hypothesis – has it that the universe has existed pretty much in its present state forever, with the density of matter being neither greater nor less than it is right now. The other hypothesis – the 'Big Bang' hypothesis – has it that the universe began in an enormous explosion known as the Big Bang, and since then matter has been moving further and further apart. The group considers the evidence and admits that it does not yet favour either hypothesis over the other. As the group members put it, the probability of one hypothesis is at present equal to the probability of the other. Here the word 'probability' does *not* mean what it means when we say 'The probability of being left-handed if you were born in Derby is 20%'. It isn't, in other words, a way of providing statistical information. It means simply that we are no more certain of the truth of one hypothesis than we are of the truth of the other.

But then a new piece of evidence arrives, the detection of a strange background radiation that is entirely explicable in terms of the Big Bang hypothesis but entirely mysterious if the Steady State hypothesis is true. The probabilities now shift towards the Big Bang theory, so that that theory is more probable than the Steady State. (Though some members of the group are inclined to dispute this.)

Now let's put the clock back to the early 1800s, and a group of natural historians (whom we would now call biologists) is considering two hypotheses about a striking phenomenon: the fact that different species are perfectly adapted to survival in their separate habitats. One hypothesis has it that they were made that way by a benevolent creator. The other hypothesis has it that it was a result of wholly natural forces of some unspecified kind. Considering these two, the group is entirely at a loss to imagine just what wholly natural forces, blind and impartial as they are, could possibly have resulted in this perfect adaptation. For this group, then, the probabilities are clearly on the side of the creator hypothesis. But then, mid-century, a new theory emerges which fills in the gaps with the astonishing proposal that variations between species emerge initially as a result of random forces, but those variations that, by chance, lead to a better fit with the demands and opportunities of the environment are then preserved by a process of natural selection. The organisms that are better able to survive are more likely to have offspring, which therefore preserve their adaptive characteristics. This now shifts the probabilities, perhaps to the half-way mark. Now the benevolent creator hypothesis is no more probable than the natural selection hypothesis. (Again, however, some members of the group dispute this.)

We needn't worry about the historical accuracy of these little sketches. The point is just to illustrate a kind of agnosticism which we may call 'evidential agnosticism'. It is appropriate in cases where we are contemplating a hypothesis (especially a scientific hypothesis) which is capable of being supported, or refuted, by evidence. When the evidence does not yet settle the matter, we are agnostic about the truth of the hypothesis.

How does evidential agnosticism relate to weak and strong agnosticism? Well, if we are strong agnostics about a hypothesis – if we think we could *never* be in a position to establish whether that hypothesis is true or not – then we have to be evidential agnostics too: we have to admit that the evidence does not settle it (and neither does any other consideration). But, curiously, you could be an evidential agnostic without being a weak agnostic. You could think that the *evidence* doesn't settle the matter of God's existence one way or another, but still not be in any doubt as to God's existence. You may think, that is, that knowing that God exists is not a matter of having conclusive, or even persuasive, evidence in favour of a hypothesis. Belief in God, you may point out, is not belief in a *hypothesis*, any more than belief that there is a world out there in front of us is a hypothesis: it is simply a belief we cannot help having. The idea of bringing evidence to bear on it is just not appropriate. So, at any rate, you might be inclined to argue.

Dawkins' distinction

Evidential agnosticism corresponds to the position Richard Dawkins describes as *Temporary Agnosticism in Practice* (TAP). Notice the optimism implied by the 'temporary': we hope that, sooner or later, we will discover the evidence we need to settle the issue, and once we have it, such agnosticism evaporates. He contrasts this with *Permanent Agnosticism in Principle* (PAP). Here, there is no hope of discovering the crucial evidence for or against the hypothesis, because

> the very idea of evidence is not applicable. The question exists on a different plane, or in a different dimension, beyond the zones that evidence can reach. An example might be that philosophical chestnut, the question whether you see red as I do. Maybe your red is my green, or something completely different from any colour I can imagine.

It's tempting to identify PAP with what we have called strong agnosticism, but it may be better to think of PAP as one version of it. Two kinds of reasons justify strong agnosticism: either the idea of evidence is just inapplicable (and PAP is the right attitude), or it is applicable, but the evidence is mixed, and will inescapably remain so. That second reason would lead us to a permanent evidential agnosticism.

Dawkins invites us to consider a scale of attitudes, ranging from category 1, those who think it 100% probable that God exists, to category 7, those who think it 100% probable that he doesn't. He puts himself in category 6, 'but leaning towards 7'. Subscribers to TAP belong in the middle region of, though not a specific point on, this scale, but PAP agnostics belong nowhere on it, because the matters on which we are obliged to be PAP-ists cannot be given any probability rating. Again, the probabilities are intended just as indications of degrees of certainty, but Dawkins' choice of the term 'probability' suggests that what should determine the reasonable position on the scale is the evidence available. He goes on to point out, however, that many of those in category 1 hold on to their position as a matter of faith rather than reason. A scale that was based solely on probability-as-determined-by-evidence-alone would have some theists, perhaps most, somewhere in the middle.

For Dawkins, the question of the existence of God is a scientific hypothesis, and so any agnosticism about it will be in the TAP category (genuinely scientific questions being ones we can in principle answer). But, he argues, given what we now know about the origins of the human race and of the origins of religious belief, agnosticism is no longer justified. Should we agree? We'll be tackling this later. But first, an historical interlude.

Chapter 2
Who were the first agnostics?

There are two ways of approaching this question. The first is to ask who were the first to *call* themselves 'agnostics'. The answer to that is straightforward: the biologist Thomas Henry Huxley (1825–95); the father of Virginia Woolf and one-time priest Leslie Stephen (1832–1904); and the philosopher Herbert Spencer (1820–1903). The second way of approaching the question is to ask who originated the *idea* of agnosticism, under whatever name, and that question is not so easy to answer. Huxley, Stephen, and Spencer were all influenced by earlier writers, and it is possible to trace a concern with the limits of human knowledge through virtually the whole history of philosophy, science, and religion. In telling (briefly and very incompletely) the story, we will begin with the first of those eminent Victorians, and then move further backwards in time from them.

Thomas Henry Huxley and the Metaphysical Society

One November evening in 1868 at 'The Hollies', his house on Clapham Common, James Knowles, editor of the periodical *Nineteenth Century*, was entertaining his old headmaster Charles Pritchard and the poet Alfred Tennyson. Knowles proposed the formation of a theological society, the purpose of which would be to discuss religious issues with the same impartiality and open-mindedness that characterized scientific discussions. Receiving from the others an undertaking that they would join such a group, Knowles extended invitations to individuals covering a wide range of religious outlooks. One of these was Dr Stanley, dean of Westminster. Stanley, however, thought an exclusive concentration on theological matters was too narrow, and would do little to close the growing gulf between science and religion. Stanley's wife, Lady Augusta, then suggested that the group be called the Metaphysical Society, and the suggestion was adopted. The membership was then widened to bring in scientists, philosophers, and politicians, including the prime minister, William Ewart Gladstone.

Among these early members of the Society was Thomas Henry Huxley, by then a well-known scientist and public lecturer. Having studied medicine, he had spent four years as assistant surgeon on *HMS Rattlesnake*, was appointed lecturer at the Royal School of Mines in 1854, and subsequently Fullerian Professor of Physiology at the Royal Institution. Huxley is best known today for his championship of Darwin's theory of natural selection. Unlike Darwin, who was a retiring man, he was a very active and effective public speaker and reached a wide audience through his lectures and numerous writings in popular periodicals. His tenacious defence of Darwinism earned him the nickname 'Darwin's Bulldog'.

Among the members of the Metaphysical Society, Huxley became aware that, although the range of opinions represented was diverse, everyone else seemed to have some definite outlook on the world that could often be captured in a single word: positivism, materialism, theism, and so on. Huxley wondered what name would describe his own position. The trouble was that no existing word quite did the job – every term he alighted on indicated a level of confidence he did not feel. It then struck him that what defined his outlook was precisely this *lack of certainty*. As it yet had no name, he invented one: agnosticism. (Or perhaps

3. An intimate portrait of 'Darwin's Bulldog' and the inventor of the term 'agnosticism', Thomas Henry Huxley

he recalled the word 'agnostic' from a letter written ten years earlier from Isabel Arundell, wife of the explorer Sir Richard Burton.)

Two stories were told of how Huxley came to choose this name. According to a letter by the editor of the *Spectator* Richard Hutton (subsequently quoted in the 1888 edition of what became the *Oxford English Dictionary*), the name had been suggested to Huxley by the following passage in the New Testament, relating a visit by St Paul to Athens:

> Then Paul stood in the midst of Mars' hill, and said, Ye men of Athens, I perceive that in all things ye are too superstitious.
>
> For as I passed by, and beheld your devotions, I found an altar with this inscription, TO THE UNKNOWN GOD. Whom therefore ye ignorantly worship, him I declare unto you.

In the Greek New Testament, the phrase 'to the unknown God' appears as '*agnosto theo*'.

But according to Huxley's own account of the matter, published 20 years after he had first coined the term in 1869, his intention was to draw a contrast between his own uncertainty and the claims to secret and privileged knowledge that characterized the *gnostics*. The original gnostics were a religious sect, predating Christianity, which claimed a special understanding of the nature and will of God. Later, this combined with Christianity to produce a group (a fringe group, as some would see it) who distinguished themselves from ordinary Christians by belief in an elevated understanding of the gospels inherited from the disciples and ultimately from Jesus himself. Huxley detected a similar tendency towards gnosticism when he contemplated some of his theistic contemporaries. He, in contrast, was an *a*-gnostic, a non-gnostic.

The word spreads

Huxley tells us that he took 'the earliest opportunity of parading' the new word at a meeting of the Metaphysical Society. But although he may have paraded it in conversation, he did not do so in print for a number of years, and most of those who used the term from 1869 onwards did not know that it had been invented by Huxley. His own first published use of the word was in his book on Hume, which appeared in 1878, nine years after he had first thought of the term. By then, it was common currency, thanks mainly to the efforts of editors of popular journals. One of these was Richard Hutton, who wrote many articles on the subject in the pages of the *Spectator*. In an article entitled 'Pope Huxley', Hutton describes Huxley as 'a great and even severe Agnostic, who goes about exhorting all men to know how little they know'. James Knowles also contributed to the spread of the word through his periodical, the *Nineteenth Century*. Other popular periodicals in which the name appeared were *Leisure Hour*, *Fraser's Magazine*, *Notes and Queries*, and the *Westminster Review*. The theme was also taken up in religious periodicals such as the *Theological Review* and the *Church Quarterly Review*.

One of the first people to publicly declare themselves as agnostic was Huxley's friend Leslie Stephen, who in 1876 published *An Agnostic's Apology*. Stephen had grown up in a devoutly Christian home, took holy orders in 1855, and the following year was elected to a fellowship of his Cambridge college, Trinity Hall. Within five years, however, he was experiencing religious doubts, the severity of which led him, by one account, to contemplate taking his own life. By 1862, he felt unable to conduct college services, and a few years later resigned his fellowship. After a period in the United States, he settled in London, where he became editor of the *Cornhill Magazine*, and the first editor of the *Dictionary of National Biography*. He was knighted in 1902. *An Agnostic's Apology* makes it clear how far he had moved away from his earlier religious beliefs, dismissing theological debate as empty word-play. But although he professed himself unable to reconcile belief in a just God with the existence of suffering, he did not think of himself as an atheist.

Agnosticism from an Oxford pulpit

Although Church leaders were quick to level against agnosticism the charge that it was just another name for atheism, one of the first people whom Huxley identified as an ally was a prominent churchman, Henry Longueville Mansel, on the basis of Mansel's 1858 Bampton Lectures in Oxford, delivered from the pulpit of St Mary's, the University Church. The Bampton Lectureship had been established by the Revd John Bampton in 1780 for the purpose of defending Christian doctrine. In the light of the founder's intentions, the theme of the 1858 lectures, 'The Limits of Religious Thought', was a rather daring one. The lectures were a huge success, and the following year, Mansel was appointed Waynflete Professor of Moral and Metaphysical Philosophy at Oxford. In 1866, he moved to the Regius Chair of Ecclesiastical History, and in 1868, just three years before his death, he became dean of St Paul's in London.

Mansel's message was a mixture of orthodoxy and (though he would not have seen it this way) subversion. God, as a transcendent being, stands beyond the limits of human knowledge, which is only finite. So for us, God is unknowable. But he has nevertheless communicated his will to man, and these communications are preserved in the scriptures. The scriptures therefore are beyond criticism, and our faith must be guided by them.

It might seem that these two lines of thought – the finitude and fallibility of human thought and the infallibility of the scriptures – are in tension with one another. If the scriptures are the work of man, and man is fallible, then the scriptures themselves are fallible. How can we be sure that they convey any truths about God? And if they do convey such truths, then don't we have knowledge of God after all? Mansel, however, avoids

The Christ Church Express No 2   Tuesday.

4. An agnostic clergyman? Henry Longueville Mansel (far left), entertains his friends at Christ Church, Oxford

inconsistency through his theory of *regulative truth*. The scriptures are divinely inspired, so they give us a direct route to God's intentions, but what they reveal is not God's true nature, but the way in which God wants us to conceive of him. The words of scripture and theology are *regulative*: they set the boundaries of what we should and should not think of God, and how we should behave in response. But they are not literally true of him. The moment we try to conceive of what God must be like in himself, as opposed to how he reveals himself to man, we end up in paradox and confusion. We must be content with appearances alone. That was Mansel's distinctive version of negative theology.

When he read Mansel's lectures, Huxley was enthusiastic, not so much about the defence of scripture, but about what Mansel said concerning human knowledge, and he recommended them to others. Another ten years were to pass, however, before he found a label for the position he detected in *The Limits of Religious Thought*.

Setting the record straight: the agnostic principle

It is a curious fact that between 1869 and 1883, a period when discussion of agnosticism was at its height, Huxley did not reveal in print that he was the originator of the word. Why this long silence? He was, apparently, quite happy for it to be promoted by others, such as Richard Hutton, perhaps thinking that by those means it would more effectively be impressed on the public consciousness. In his own account of the matter he hints that, had it been known from the first that the term originated with him, it would have met with some suspicion.

Eventually, he was tricked into a public confession by the editor of a new journal called *The Agnostic Annual*. Replying to a letter from its editor, Charles Watts, Huxley acknowledged his parentage of the word, but, believing this to be an entirely private correspondence, was outraged when Watts published his letter in the first issue of the journal.

Not long after this, however, Huxley had reason to go public. He found himself being identified with two opposing positions. On the one hand, there was the complaint by churchmen and others that agnosticism was no more than a cover for atheism, and could only undermine religion. Prominent among these complainants was Dr Henry Wace, principal of King's College, London, who referred to agnostics as 'infidels'. On the other hand, Huxley was often grouped together with Herbert Spencer, who had argued for the real existence of an unknowable 'Absolute', something that sounded suspiciously like God. Huxley even found agnosticism being presented as something like a religion, a creed, albeit a somewhat negative one, with its own articles of faith. It seemed that agnosticism really was taking on the character of the beliefs St Paul detected amongst the Athenians. Finally, in 1889, he decided to set the record straight. In 'Agnosticism and Christianity', he wrote:

> Agnosticism is not properly described as a 'negative' creed, nor indeed as a creed of any kind, except in so far as it expresses absolute faith in the validity of a principle, which is as much ethical and intellectual. This principle may be stated in various ways, but they all amount to this: that it is wrong for a man to say that he is certain of the objective truth of any proposition unless he can produce evidence which logically justifies that certainty. This is what Agnosticism asserts: and, in my opinion, it is all that is essential to Agnosticism.

Later, he adds:

> I do not very much care to speak of anything as 'unknowable'.

In these belated remarks, Huxley is attempting to rid his own term of the various connotations that had been attached to it by the writings of others and in the mind of the public. But it was something of a losing battle, and by the time he wrote these words, the *Oxford English Dictionary* had already defined 'agnostic' as 'one who holds that the evidence of anything beyond and behind material phenomena is unknown and (so far as can be judged) unknowable'.

Huxley defies characterization in the terms we introduced in the previous chapter. He is not a strong agnostic, since he does not go so far as to say that we cannot have knowledge of God's existence and nature. But if he is a weak agnostic, his is a weak agnosticism that is based on principle, the principle never to claim certainty for anything for which one does not have adequate justification: this is the *agnostic principle*.

The unknowability of the noumenal: Immanuel Kant

In coming to the views expressed in his Bampton Lectures, Mansel was heavily influenced by the German philosopher Immanuel Kant (1724–1804). Very few in Mansel's audience at St Mary's would have been familiar with Kant's work. His writings present formidable difficulties to anyone who wishes to understand his outlook, but those who have made the effort to read them carefully judge him to be one of the greatest thinkers of all time. His reflections on knowledge make him an essential part of any history of agnosticism.

Kant lived all his life in Königsberg (now Kaliningrad), then part of the Prussian Empire. He taught at the university for many years as a *privatdozent*, which was an unsalaried post, and was rewarded for his patience when he was elected, at the age of 56, to the chair of Logic and Metaphysics, a post he held until he was 72. By the time he was appointed to this prestigious position, he had written books on mathematics and physics, as well as philosophy. But he now devoted himself to philosophy, and it was during his occupancy of this chair, a time many people would then have considered the autumn of their lives, when he published the works for which he is best known: the *Critique of Pure Reason* (1781) and the *Critique of Practical Reason* (1788).

In the first of these, Kant offers his response to the two main theories of knowledge: empiricism, dominant in Britain at the time, and rationalism, which was dominant on the Continent. Empiricism holds that the source of knowledge of the world is derived entirely from sensory experience. Rationalism, in contrast, holds that it is possible to gain knowledge purely through the exercise of the mind. Both of these approaches, thinks Kant, are mistaken. Empiricism is mistaken because, although experience may be the *occasion* of our acquiring knowledge, it cannot be the sole *source* of knowledge because pure experience (if there could be

5. The Königsberg professor who sought to demonstrate how, in a world almost wholly unknown to us, our moral sense can nevertheless lead us to God: Immanuel Kant

such a thing) would be completely uninterpretable. The mind must impose categories of thought on experience before it can be made intelligible, and these categories are not independent of reason. On the other hand, pure reason cannot give us knowledge either, and attempts to establish truths about the world on the basis of reason alone result in contradiction. Kant provides a dramatic demonstration of this in his 'Four Antinomies of Pure Reason' in the first *Critique*: each antinomy consists of two arguments, set side by side, for contradictory conclusions. The result is that we are seemingly compelled to think contradictory things of the world. The First Antinomy concerns the spatial and temporal boundaries of the world: that the world had a beginning in time *and* that it did not; and that the world is spatially finite in extent *and* that it is not. The Second concerns the structure of objects: that objects are ultimately composed of simple objects, which have no parts, *and* that there are no such simple objects. The Third concerns freedom: that we are free *and* that we are bound by iron laws of causality. And the Fourth concerns the existence of a supreme being: that there exists a being whose existence is (unlike ours) absolutely necessary *and* that there is no such being. No wonder metaphysics, that branch of philosophy which is supposed to tell us the true nature of reality, is mired in controversy!

What is the solution to this conundrum? Do we have *any* knowledge at all? The solution, suggests Kant, is to recognize, firstly, that knowledge is limited to objects of possible experience – what Kant describes as the *phenomenal* world; and secondly, that the structures reason uses to make experience intelligible – structures like space and time – do not belong to things independently of our experience of them. This realm beyond experience is the *noumenal* world. Of this realm we can say nothing, perhaps not even whether or not it exists, though we can perhaps say what it is *not* like.

Where does this leave God? He can't be part of the phenomenal world because God is supposed to transcend all experience. And contemplating the Fourth Antinomy, on a necessary being, we might expect Kant to say that God is one of those structures of thought that we can't help imposing on our understanding of the world, but which does not correspond to anything in the noumenal world (if it is even legitimate to talk of the existence of the noumenal world). We do not come to God through sensory experience, and we do not come to him through pure reason either. There have been attempts to establish the existence of God by rational argument alone, but Kant, having usefully categorized these attempts, goes on to show that they all fail. Altogether, theology does not look in good shape by the end of the first *Critique*.

But Kant has not yet spoken of morality, and this he does in the second *Critique*. We recognize within ourselves an awareness of what Kant calls the *categorical imperative*. Some things strike us as the right thing to do *if* we want to achieve certain aims: these he describes as *hypothetical* imperatives. But the categorical imperative does not depend in this way on particular goals that may vary from person to person: what it requires us to do is right absolutely, without qualification. And it is this categorical imperative that takes us to God, for God is the divine lawgiver.

Is Kant an agnostic? There is a case for thinking of him as a kind of agnostic: he is concerned to draw the limits of knowledge, and he draws them rather more tightly than our common sense would have done. Of the world beyond experience, he says, we can know nothing. This is an agnosticism about the nature, and perhaps even the existence, of the noumenal world. But he is not agnostic about God, though his belief about God has nothing to do with the *evidence* that the world provides for God's existence. Kant's God, however, seems a rather abstract thing, not wholly distinct from the moral law itself. Whatever else is part of God's nature is closed to us.

Kant, then, is a rather ambiguous figure as far as our list of historical agnostics is concerned, but it was Kant who helped Mansel, Huxley, and Spencer towards their agnostic conclusions.

David Hume and his Fork

One of the British empiricists to whom Kant was responding was David Hume (1711–76). It was reading Hume, says Kant, that 'interrupted my dogmatic slumber' – a reference to Hume's tendency to undermine claims to knowledge in certain areas of thought. Here, then, is another significant figure in the story of agnosticism.

Unlike Kant, Hume was never a professional philosopher, though he made an attempt to become one, in 1745, when he applied for the chair of Ethics and Pneumatical Philosophy (now Moral Philosophy) at Edinburgh. Another opportunity came in 1752 when the chair of Logic at Glasgow fell vacant. Both times, however, his appointment was opposed by those who objected to the anti-religious views they detected in his writings, notably the *Treatise of Human Nature*, written when he was just 25. In fact, the *Treatise* mentions God only in passing, but (as Hume was well aware) it challenges ordinary beliefs concerning causation which might be thought essential to our understanding of God.

Though denied an academic position, Hume had a varied career, first (and briefly) as a clerk in a firm of sugar merchants, then as tutor to a young nobleman (later declared insane), then as an army officer, librarian to the Faculty of Advocates at Edinburgh, secretary to the British ambassador in Paris, and finally as a civil servant in London. His writings are similarly varied, including political works and a history of Britain.

Two theses are central to Hume's philosophy. The first is his empiricism: all our ideas have their ultimate source in impressions: perceptions, sensations, and emotions. For every simple idea – that is, one that cannot be decomposed into other ideas – there must be a corresponding impression. More complex ideas can then be built up from these simple ones. The second thesis has come to be known as 'Hume's Fork': that all the possible objects of our knowledge can be divided into two kinds, *relations of ideas* and *matters of fact*. Examples of matters of fact would include the following: there is a tree in the garden, there is a storm raging, all the people in this room are right-handed. Matters of

31

6. **Drawing the limits of human knowledge: David Hume, philosopher, historian, librarian, and civil servant**

fact concern states of affairs in the world, the world being one that we could conceive to be otherwise than it is: there might have been no trees in the garden, the weather might have been fair, and there might have been a left-handed person in this room. In contrast, relations of ideas concern things that could *not* have been otherwise: the square root of 36 is 6, anything with weight occupies space, all bipeds have two feet, and so on. Relations of ideas concern, not how the world is, but the content of our concepts, which we can discern just by inspecting them.

The combination of these two theses – the dependence of our concepts on experience and the distinction between matters of fact and relations of ideas – leads to some surprising results. Hume says, plausibly, that all our reasonings concerning matters of fact depend on the relation between cause and effect. But what is this relation? How do we become aware of it? As we ordinarily conceive of it, it is a kind of necessary connection between events. Causes are not merely arbitrarily juxtaposed with their effects: they *make those effects happen*. But where, asks Hume, does this idea of necessary connection come from? Necessity is something we associate with relations of ideas. But *this* kind of necessity – what we now call 'logical necessity' – is not to be found in causal truths. For I can conceive, without absurdity, a lightning flash not being followed by the clap of thunder it normally causes. Causes, then, are not logically tied to their effects. Is the relevant kind of necessary connection to be found in experience, then? No. As far as our perception of causation goes, all we perceive is the effect following the cause. Of course, not all succession is causation: there must be a constant conjunction between events before we recognize a causal connection. This still does not amount to necessity. However, the constant conjunction leads to a certain disposition in our minds: an expectation, when we perceive the cause, that the effect will follow. It is this *psychological* compulsion that is the source of the idea of necessary connection. But, not recognizing it as the source, we project the compulsion onto the events themselves, thus illustrating, as Hume puts it, the mind's 'great propensity to spread itself on external objects'.

Hume's deflating of the idea of causal necessity, and the general view of knowledge that prompted it, are likely to spell trouble for religious belief. The notion of God as something really existing in the world, though not a direct object of experience, as something that exists of necessity rather than accidentally, the ultimate cause of things, on which all else necessarily depends – all this is vulnerable to Hume's view of the limits of human knowledge. It is not surprising, then, that when Hume discusses religion, he is critical of it, sometimes in his own voice, as when he exposes the irrationality of belief in miracles, and sometimes in the guise of a fictional character, as in his *Dialogues Concerning Natural Religion*, in which one of the participants, Philo, launches a devastating attack on arguments for the existence of God.

Hume's Fork – the distinction between matters of fact and relations and ideas – has been enormously influential, and led ultimately to the 20th-century movement known as logical positivism, which itself had a transformative effect on philosophical views of religion, as we shall see in Chapter 5.

Is Hume an agnostic? Huxley clearly saw him as a kindred spirit, describing him as 'the parent of Kant and...the protagonist of that more modern way of thinking which has been called "agnosticism"'. In Huxley's terms, Hume is indeed an agnostic, in that he clearly draws the limits of knowledge and shows just what knowledge claims turn out to be unfounded. On the specific issue of the existence of God, however, he is often thought of as an atheist, and his occasional concessions to religion therefore merely ironic. And contemplating the devastating eloquence of some of the passages in the *Dialogues*, it is hard not to believe that they were written by someone who had entirely rejected religious belief as irrational. Look, for example, at this unforgettable passage, where Philo (whom some identify with Hume) comments on Cleanthes' argument from the marks of design in the universe to a divine designer, whose intellect and capacity for autonomous action is analogous, though far superior, to our own:

In a word, Cleanthes, a man who follows your hypothesis is able, perhaps, to assert or conjecture that the universe sometime arose from something like design; but beyond that position he cannot ascertain one single circumstance, and is left afterwards to fix every point of his theology by the utmost license of fancy and hypothesis. This world, for aught he knows, is very faulty and imperfect, compared to a superior standard, and was only the first rude essay of some infant deity who afterwards abandoned it, ashamed of his lame performance; it is the work only of some dependent, inferior deity, and is the object of derision to his superiors; it is the production of old age and dotage in some superannuated deity, and ever since his death has run on at adventures, from the first impulse and active force which it received from him.... From the moment the attributes of the Deity are supposed finite, all these have place. And I cannot, for my part, think that so wild and unsettled a system of theology is, in any respect, preferable to none at all.

Nevertheless, an outright denial of the existence of God would have gone beyond the limits Hume had set for knowledge. Perhaps the order we observe in nature does not point unerringly to a benevolent and all-powerful creator, but Philo (and perhaps also Hume) is prepared to concede that the universe may have been produced by something that bears some analogy to human intelligence. Vague though this is, it certainly does not shut the door on theism.

The followers of Pyrrho

Just as Kant was influenced by Hume, so Hume was influenced by a group of Greek philosophers known as 'Pyrrhonists' or Pyrrhonian sceptics, named after Pyrrho, who lived from around 365 to around 270 BC. He was originally a painter, but became a philosopher, travelled with his teacher to India and there met the 'gymno-sophists', whose attainment of a state of contemplative tranquillity greatly impressed him. Returning to Greece, he took a number of pupils, who passed on his views to later generations (Pyrrho himself left no writings). According to one pupil, Timon,

Pyrrho taught that knowledge of things is impossible and that the recognition of this, with the consequent suspension of belief, will lead ultimately to *ataraxia*: a state of calmness and contentment. As a school of thought, however, Pyrrhonism was founded in the 1st century BC.

The most important source of our knowledge of ancient scepticism is the work of the physician and philosopher Sextus Empiricus, who flourished around AD 200. His writings were for a time lost, but then rediscovered in the 16th century. In *Outlines of Pyrrhonism*, Sextus explains what it is to be a sceptic, contrasting sceptics with two other kinds of philosopher: the dogmatists, who think they have found knowledge, and the academic philosophers, who think it cannot be found. In contrast, the sceptics, realizing that they have not found knowledge yet, are compelled to keep searching. This is strikingly reminiscent of Huxley's contrast between the gnostics, who felt that they had a special route to understanding, people like Spencer, who believed in the existence of the unknowable, and true agnostics like himself, who recognized their own lack of knowledge but hesitated to describe anything as unknowable.

So what is scepticism? Sextus tells us that it is

> an ability to set out oppositions among things which appear and are thought of in any way at all, an ability by which, because of the equipollence in the opposed objects and accounts, we come first to suspension of judgement and afterwards to tranquillity.

What he means by 'opposition' here is that, for any reason inclining us to form a given belief, we can find another reason for the opposite belief. These opposing reasons are equal in power or persuasive force, the result being that, not knowing which belief to adopt, we suspend our belief altogether. Sextus makes this state sound rather agreeable, however: it does not seem to be one we would work hard to get out of. So we might wonder about his characterization of the sceptics as those who are still searching. Again, Sextus's picture of the methods of the sceptic reminds us of a parallel with later discussion, this time between the sceptic's use of opposing reasons and Kant's antinomies of pure reason. But whereas the sceptic suspends judgement, Kant takes the antinomies to show that the world itself cannot be the way it is represented on either side of the antinomy. For example, it has neither a beginning in time nor an infinite past, because it is not temporal at all.

Sextus sets out a number of 'modes', or ways of arguing, which illustrate these oppositions, remarking, however, that he does not necessarily endorse them all. In many cases, he is simply reporting the arguments of his predecessors, those who were active during the heyday of Pyrrhonian scepticism. Some of these arguments concern the relativity of perception: how the world appears to us in perception depends on which species we belong to (since this determines the means we have of perceiving the world – compare humans, bees, and bats, for example), the state of our sense organs, our powers of discernment, whether we are ill or healthy, and whether we are near to or far from the object perceived. We cannot, then, trust our senses to intimate how things truly are, as opposed to how they appear to us on particular occasions.

Another sceptical manoeuvre reported by Sextus is the regress of reasons. We may take a belief to be well founded because we have a reason for that belief. But that reason, if we are to regard it as adequate grounds for belief, must itself be justified by a further reason. That further reason must be supported by yet another reason, and so on *ad infinitum*. Since, as finite beings, we cannot possibly provide an infinite chain of reasons, it follows that no belief is ultimately well founded.

Sextus also presents us with a series of arguments directed at specific aspects of our conception of the world. Change, motion, coming into and going out of existence, space, time, and number:

each of these, it is argued, involve us in contradiction. Consider time, for example. It is divided into past, present, and future. Are these divisions themselves divisible? Past and future seem to be, but what of the present? If it is divisible, then it must have parts that are past or future, and so not present, which is absurd. But if it is not divisible, then nothing can change in the present, for change itself is divisible into earlier and later parts, and so therefore must any time in which change occurs. About the nature of time, therefore, we have to suspend judgement.

What about God? If we have a conception of God, then we ought to be able to say what his properties are. But, says Sextus, there is no agreement about this. Some dogmatists say that he has a body, others that he doesn't; some that he is in space, others that he is outside it; some that he is like a human, others unlike, and so on. But since every property of God is in dispute, how can we say that we have any conception of him? Moreover, it cannot be obvious that he exists, for if it was, then we would not be in any doubt as to his nature. Clearly, then, the existence of God stands in need of proof. But if the proof starts from a premise which is indisputable, and moves by obviously correct means to the conclusion, then it would be obvious that he existed. So the proof must either start from something disputable, or uses disputable means to get to the conclusion, in which case it requires further support, and once more we are embarked on an infinite regress. So the existence of God is not obvious, and we can neither prove nor disprove his existence.

It looks, then, as if Sextus is an agnostic, and this is hardly surprising, for isn't a sceptic bound to be an agnostic? In fact, now we think about it, aren't 'scepticism' and 'agnosticism' just different names for suspension of judgement?

There certainly is a connection between agnosticism and scepticism, but there are also important differences. To be an agnostic is to recognize that one does not have adequate grounds for claims to knowledge, or (more radically) for belief. For Sextus, to be a sceptic is to be able to show that any reasons for belief are matched by corresponding reasons for the contrary belief. These are not quite the same. We might put the contrast like this: agnosticism is a state of mind; scepticism a method. And in so far as scepticism leads to agnosticism, we might say that scepticism is the cause and agnosticism the effect. (Or perhaps we should say that scepticism is *a* cause, as there is more than one route to agnosticism.) In addition, most agnosticism is what we called in the previous chapter 'local' agnosticism, whereas sceptical arguments tend to be fairly wide-ranging.

Of course, the terms can be used more loosely, and when they are, they will be harder to disentangle. But we can perhaps see why Huxley did not choose to call himself a sceptic, for the kind of extreme scepticism represented by the followers of Pyrrho would have been far too strong for his purposes, undermining science as well as religion. To have described himself publicly as a sceptic would have put him beyond the pale in the intellectual circles in which he moved.

Chapter 3
Is agnosticism necessary?

The dragon and the teapot

In *The Demon-Haunted World*, the American cosmologist and writer Carl Sagan (1934–96) imagines the following conversation between himself and the reader following his announcement that a fire-breathing dragon lives in his garage:

> 'Show me,' you say. I lead you to my garage. You look inside and see a ladder, empty paint cans, an old tricycle – but no dragon.
>
> 'Where's the dragon?' you ask.
>
> 'Oh, she's right here,' I reply, waving vaguely. 'I neglected to mention that she's an invisible dragon.'
>
> You propose spreading flour on the floor of the garage to capture the dragon's footprints.
>
> 'Good idea,' I say, 'but this dragon floats in the air.'
>
> Then you'll use an infrared sensor to detect the invisible fire.
>
> 'Good idea, but the invisible fire is also heatless.'
>
> You'll spray-paint the dragon and make her visible.
>
> 'Good idea, except she's an incorporeal dragon and the paint won't stick.'

No matter what is proposed as a test of the dragon's presence, there's a reason why it will fail to produce a positive result. Is it reasonable to believe that there is a dragon there? Not in the absence of any convincing reasons, obviously. But then Sagan imagines other people reporting dragons in their garages, of the flour test revealing footprints, though unfortunately they only appear when no sceptic is around. Other evidence is offered, but it is always equivocal: other explanations of positive results are readily available. '[T]he only sensible approach', says Sagan, 'is tentatively to reject the dragon hypothesis, to be open to future physical data, and to wonder what the cause might be that so many apparently sane and sober people share the same strange delusion.'

Sagan does not, as one might have suspected from reading this passage, draw an explicit parallel with belief in God. His aim in the book is rather to counter the insidious and seductive influence of superstition and pseudo-science, and to contrast it with the humanizing and genuinely revelatory offerings of true science. However, the atheist philosopher Bertrand Russell (1872–1970) does draw a religious parallel when he introduces the idea of an object for which there is no positive evidence. In *Is There a God?*, he writes:

> Many orthodox people speak as though it were the business of sceptics to disprove received dogmas rather than of dogmatists to prove them. This is, of course, a mistake. If I were to suggest that between the Earth and Mars there is a china teapot revolving about the sun in a elliptical orbit, no-one would be able disprove my assertion provided I were careful to add that the teapot is too small to be revealed even by our most powerful telescopes. But if I were to go on to say that, since my assertion cannot be disproved, it would be intolerable presumption on the part of human reason to doubt it, I should rightly be thought to be talking nonsense.

What morals should we draw from the dragon and the teapot? Here are three unexceptional ones:

1) The fact that we cannot prove that there is no dragon and no teapot does not make it reasonable to suppose that they exist.

2) The fact that we cannot prove that there is no dragon and no teapot does not make it *un*reasonable to suppose that they do *not* exist.

3) The fact that we cannot prove that there is no dragon and no teapot does not make the likelihood of their existing equal to the likelihood of their not existing.

This third moral is one lesson that Dawkins draws from Russell's teapot. He also wants to draw a stronger one:

4) Whereas we cannot positively rule out the teapot (and, we might add, the dragon) with 100% certainty, it is reasonable to suppose the likelihood of its existing to be very small, or at least, much less than the probability of its existing.

That, too, seems unexceptionable, but it is worth pausing to look at the reasoning that lies behind it. For Russell, the correct attitude towards the teapot is this:

5) The onus is on defenders of the teapot (dragon) to establish their position. The initial assumption, which requires no defence, is that it does not exist, and we need positive reasons to move us away from this assumption.

So the initial probability of the teapot/dragon existing is zero, or at least very small. Why would anyone just suppose there to be such a thing? That may shift as further evidence comes in, but it would need to be quite impressive evidence for that probability to overtake the probability of a non-existent teapot/dragon.

Putting these various thoughts together, we arrive at the overall moral Dawkins draws from Russell:

6) Theism is in a similar position to belief in the teapot (dragon). The fact that we cannot prove that there is no God is a very weak argument in favour of an agnosticism that takes God's existing to

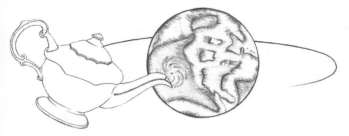

7. Unseen and undetected: Russell's celestial teapot

be as probable as his not existing. And if allowing more than 0% probability to God's existing counts as agnosticism (because it leaves some room for doubt, however little), then we should be teapot agnostics, too.

Clearly, we are entitled to our belief that neither the teapot nor the dragon exists, and we don't have to offer convincing reasons for our belief other than that we haven't been given any good reasons for thinking that they *do* exist. And if the analogy with God is a fair one, then we no more need to make room for agnosticism about God than we need to make room for agnosticism about invisible dragons and teapots.

At this point, we need to ask two questions: *is* the analogy a fair one?; and is it true that the burden of proof lies on defenders of God's existence, just as the burden of proof lies on defenders of dragons in garages and teapots in space?

Is the analogy fair?

The first thing to note is that both the teapot and (initially) the dragon are described as making absolutely no difference to anything. They are as self-effacing as anything could be. No only do they not announce themselves, but nothing seems to hang on whether they exist or not. Not so God, at least as he is conceived by the great theistic religions. The God hypothesis is intended to cast light on some of the most fundamental questions we can ask:

How, if the universe came into existence, did it do so?

If it didn't come into existence, but has always existed, is there any explanation for its existence?

What, if anything, is the purpose of life?

Why do we have a moral conscience?

How can that conscience tell us what is right?

Notice how few presuppositions these questions make. We can ask them whatever our perspective, religious or non-religious. They don't presuppose that the universe *must* have an explanation, that life *does* have a purpose, and that our moral conscience puts us in touch with a distinction between right and wrong that exists quite independently of human thought and feeling. They are not loaded questions. Perhaps the right answers to them are ones that don't involve God at all. But the point is that there are apparently informative answers to them that *do* involve God. And whether or not those answers are the right ones, the fact that they are available shows that the God hypothesis is not necessarily completely redundant in the way that the teapot and dragon hypotheses clearly are.

Now, it might be thought, we can easily amend those other stories to make them highly relevant to the fundamental questions above. The two stories are just asking to be combined, so let's do so. The teapot is actually the source of all existence. On it are written all the moral laws. The dragon, with its supersensory perception, can see what is written on the teapot and coveys that information via a kind of telepathy to the humans whose garage it occupies. (Perhaps we had better imagine a dragon for every household, or every individual.) And let us, to further intrigue and beguile, add a level of metaphysical mystery to the story by the startling announcement that the dragon (or rather dragons) *is* (are) the teapot. That somehow the teapot, in all its remote crystalline beauty, is one and the same as the living dragon in the garage. Teapot is made dragon. Now we have a hypothesis that offers to solve the deepest mysteries. But it doesn't look like an alternative to the God hypothesis so much as a bizarre variant on it. The teapot-dragon *is* God incarnate. The question then is just what the teapot-ness of the teapot and the dragon-ness of the dragon add to the story. These aspects seem redundant even if we have *something* here that is not.

There is a further difference between the God hypothesis and the (unamended) dragon and teapot hypotheses. The actual existence of God, assuming him to have a particular interest in human welfare, has consequences for us that the existence of those other entities would not. There is the possibility, perhaps, of divine intervention, of certain transformative experiences, of our being given eternal life. Now, of course, although this makes the God hypothesis more significant for us, it doesn't make it any more likely to be true. There are many things that aren't true which, if they *were* true, would have the most momentous consequences for us. But, even so, it makes agnosticism about God a less redundant position than agnosticism about the teapot, as described by Russell.

Let's put the point in terms of risk assessment. When companies draw up risk assessments of various activities they are proposing to engage in, they describe possible outcomes of those activities, or external events that might impinge on them, under two heads: *likelihood* and *impact*. The occasional computer crash may be very likely, for example, but (provided it doesn't happen too often) it has very little long-term impact. Invasion by aliens from another galaxy, by contrast, would have a dramatic and possibly permanent impact, but the likelihood is treated as negligible (in fact, it would be most unlikely even to feature on a risk-assessment document unless the assessor had an uncontrollable sense of humour). Much of the discussion would no doubt centre on medium-likelihood, medium-impact situations.

Applying this to the analogy we are concerned with, a risk assessment on Russell's orbiting teapot and Sagan's dragon in the garage would rate these as low (indeed zero) impact and low probability. They just aren't worth worrying about: whether they are there or not, everything will continue just the same. Not so with the God hypothesis. Suppose, as Dawkins wants to argue, the hypothesis has a very low probability, sufficiently low indeed that, according to him, we needn't scruple to be agnostics about its truth, unless we are prepared to be agnostics about a whole host of bizarre entities. Even so, its impact is by no means negligible. Indeed, it may be absolutely huge – at least at some stage, for example after death. That marks a very significant difference between God and the teapot/dragon. It makes good sense to hedge our bets where very significant events are concerned, even if they are unlikely. So agnosticism about God is not the idle and pointless attitude that agnosticism about the teapot/dragon would be.

The presumption of atheism

It is a big advantage to atheism that it is widely regarded as the default position. This almost orthodox view goes as follows. Atheism doesn't require defence. Rather, it is up to theists to convince us that there is a God. Unless they can do so, we can remain comfortable in our disbelief. Only if they produce a really compelling argument in favour are we obliged to stir ourselves and show just where the argument fails. If there's room for doubt (and there's always room for doubt over arguments for God) then the rational thing is to be atheist. And this, of course, makes agnosticism completely redundant. For agnosticism concedes – it is integral to the position, indeed – that there is room for doubt where arguments for the existence of God are concerned. Maybe there's something in some of them – who knows? But if doubt returns us to the default setting, then that takes us to atheism, not agnosticism. This is the *presumption of atheism*.

Any practising agnostic ought to have an answer to this. And the answer is that, actually, atheism is not – or not invariably – the default position. It is the default position only if some general principle that is clearly correct says that it is the default position. So what general principle could this be? Let's look at the possibilities.

(i) The default position in any debate is *whatever both parties in the debate can agree on*: the common ground, in other words. In the debate between theist and atheist, the common ground will, obviously, be everything that appears to both of them to be true, such as the existence of the physical universe. But atheism entails nothing more than this common ground. It is the theist who wants to go beyond it and posit the existence of a transcendent being. So the default is atheism.

Reply: This line of thought might initially be tempting, but it is very definitely wrong-headed. It isn't just theism that goes beyond the common ground. Atheism does so too: it says that there exists *nothing more* in the world than what both theist and atheist could agree exists. So atheists are not excused, on these grounds, from providing reasons for their position.

(ii) The default position in any debate is the *negative position*, the one that says such-and-such is *not* the case, or that such-and-such does *not* exist. Positive assertions always need justifying. In the debate about God, theism is the positive belief (God does exist), atheism the negative one (he doesn't). So atheism is the default position.

Reply: This would be a very dangerous principle to put into practice! Everyday life requires us to have countless positive beliefs about the world, some so obvious that we barely think about them: that we have bodies that allow us to move around, that whatever we see in front of us exists, that there are other people similarly situated with whom we can communicate, and so on. But the philosophical sceptic shows us that even these beliefs can be challenged. The sceptic invites you to contemplate the following: despite appearances, your brain does not reside in a body at all, but is being kept artificially alive in the laboratory of some unhinged neuroscientist, who cunningly stimulates your brain in such a way that you have a continuous series of entirely illusory experiences, making you think that you have a body, that you can move around, that what you seem to see in front of you really is in front of you, and so on. The idea is ludicrous, of course. But can you think of a reason that enables you to rule it out completely? You cannot appeal to anything in your sensory experience, since this is entirely compatible with the sceptic's hypothesis. Is there anything else you can appeal to? It isn't clear that there is. In which case, you have to concede that you do not know for certain that the sceptic's hypothesis isn't the truth. But if you don't know that you are just a brain kept artificially alive in a laboratory, then you don't know anything that would turn out to be false on such a hypothesis – that you have arms and legs, for example. Now consider again the proposal that all positive beliefs have to be justified, and in the absence of a totally convincing justification, the negative belief is the default position. Since we cannot conclusively defeat the sceptic, we would have to concede that we should give up our belief that we have bodies that can move around, and so on. We don't want to do this, so we shouldn't accept the principle.

(iii) The default position in any debate is *whatever belief is held by the majority*. Majority beliefs do not need justification. Nowadays, theism is the minority belief, so it is theists, rather than atheists, who need to establish their position.

Reply: Is theism the minority position nowadays? Perhaps it depends on how narrowly, or broadly, we construe theism. Certainly, theistic belief is very pervasive, and there are groups, societies, and cultures in which it is in fact the *majority* view. So appealing to this principle will put the onus of proof on different sides, depending on the context – that is, depending on which group the debate happens to be conducted within. In some contexts, the onus will be on the atheist. But quite apart from the issue of whether theism is or isn't the majority view, the principle is surely a suspect one. Universally applied, it would lead to intellectual inertia. The prevailing view would tend to remain the prevailing view because it would not be thought in need of defence. It is surely a good thing for commonly held beliefs to be subject to regular scrutiny. It is a fundamental tenet of education that nothing should just be taken for granted. It is also politically suspect, marginalizing small groups. It is true that some beliefs are so bizarre that only a very small number of people hold them, and they clearly stand in need of defence, but they do so precisely because they are bizarre, not because they are held only by a small number of people.

(iv) The default position in any debate is *whichever view is less likely to be true*. The more improbable the hypothesis, the greater the need for justification. Theism is intrinsically less likely than atheism, so it stands in greater need of justification.

Reply: (A rather lengthy reply this time!) This principle looks much more reasonable than the second and third we've considered. It does not, note, put the burden of proof wholly on the theist, unless it is suggested that atheism is overwhelmingly the more probable position, with only the smallest chance being assigned to theism. But we need some means of establishing the likelihood of a hypothesis before we can apply the general principle to the particular case. What we are interested in is the intrinsic, or 'prior' probability of a hypothesis: the probability it has *before* the evidence starts to come in. And here 'probability' just means how inclined we should be to believe it, rather than the extent to which its truth is determined by external forces. In some cases, the likelihood will be settled by statistical means. I may form the hypothesis that I will throw a six on the next throw of the die. The probability of that is just one in six, since there are six possibilities altogether, of which a six is just one. Most interesting cases are less clear-cut than this, since it isn't clear just how many possibilities there are. But we can perhaps measure the prior probability of a hypothesis by *how much it rules out*. The more it rules out, the lower the prior probability. The less it rules out, the greater the prior probability. Here are two extreme examples of this. Take this hypothesis: 'Either the sun will shine in New York today or it won't.' This rules out no possibilities whatsoever, since 'it won't' covers every other relevant possibility, and the hypothesis isn't incompatible with any irrelevant ones, such as a heavy rainstorm somewhere in the Pacific. Since it rules out no possibilities, then, it has a 100% prior probability (and no evidence that comes in subsequently will change this, we might note). It is, in other words, absolutely certain. Contrast this with 'It is both the case, and *not* the case, that the sun will shine in New York today.' This rules out *every* relevant possibility. There is nothing the sun could do, or fail to do, which would make the hypothesis true. And nothing else could make it true either. But since there is no possibility whose obtaining would make it true, then the hypothesis has a prior probability of 0% (and no evidence that comes in subsequently will change this either). It is, in other words, certainly false.

Of course, all interesting hypotheses will be somewhere between these extremes. They rule out some possibilities, but not all. So they have an intermediate probability. And although we might not be able to put a number on exactly how many possibilities there are that might be relevant to a given hypothesis, we can still get a sense of whether it is the truth of the hypothesis that rules out more possibilities, or its falsehood. And one way in which we can tell is by looking at how *specific* the hypothesis is. Some hypotheses are extremely specific, for example: my wet umbrella is standing at an angle of 30° against the wall just outside the kitchen, making a pool of water 100 cm² in area on the floor. There are comparatively few ways in which this can turn out to be true, but comparatively loads of ways in which it can turn out to be false: the angle is in fact 25°, it's standing in the umbrella organizer in the porch, the area of the pool is only 60 cm², the umbrella isn't wet at all, and so on. So the prior probability of the hypothesis (again, putting aside any evidence, such as my memory of where I put it, seeing it just now, being informed of its whereabouts and current state by a witness who has generally proved reliable on such matters, and so on) is quite low – very low, in fact.

Now, with this in mind, let us take a look once more at the teapot and dragon hypotheses. Both of these are pretty specific, about the objects concerned, about their location, and about the reasons why we don't seem to have direct evidence of their existence. So each has a low prior probability, since there are, comparatively, lots of ways in which they could be false. What, then, of the God hypothesis? How specific is this? Now, this is tricky, since there is no one answer to this question. Some versions of it are more specific than others. But this is an area where one simply cannot be too specific. It would be absurd, for instance, to suppose that God wears a red bow tie with white spots. More seriously, although we may be relatively clear about the role God needs to play in the cosmos in order to be worthy of the title 'God', we would be wise to be fairly unspecific about the way in which those functions become realized.

The agnostic philosopher (and former Catholic priest) Anthony Kenny has suggested that atheism is a less modest position than theism, as it rules out more possibilities:

> Many different definitions may be offered of the word 'God'. Given this fact, atheism makes a much stronger claim than theism does. The atheist says that no matter what definition you choose, 'God exists' is always false. The theist claims only that there is some definition which makes 'God exists' true.

But atheists often object to theists of a certain stripe hijacking perfectly harmless ideas and calling them 'God'. For instance, one manoeuvre might be to take 'God' as a name for the laws of nature. But if we allow in all these non-standard forms of theism without discriminating between them, then it will be very unclear just where to locate the debate between atheists and theists. So,

51

for the purposes of this discussion, let us restrict 'theism' to the hypothesis that there exists a being who fills the following roles:

  (i) the ultimate and intentional cause of the universe's existence;
  (ii) the ultimate source of love;
(iii) the ultimate source of moral knowledge.

An alternative approach would be to list the intrinsic properties that a being must have in order to be God, such as being all-knowing, all-powerful, and so on. But such a list would be contentious. It is better to define God in terms of the role he plays, and then argue about which properties a being would have to have in order to fulfil that role. For instance, it is a reasonable inference that any being who fulfilled the roles as defined by (i)–(iii) above would have to have something at least analogous to human intelligence: in other words, to be capable of thought. For only a being capable of thought, or something like thought, could be the intentional cause of the universe's existence.

If we define God is this way, in terms of a role to be played, we can define the theism/atheism dispute in these terms: theists affirm the existence of a being who fulfils roles (i)–(iii). Atheists deny that there is one thing that fills these roles, and indeed deny that (i) is filled by anything. The universe need have no cause at all: perhaps it has always existed, extending back into the infinite past; or perhaps it came into being as a completely random event, or as a result of the death of a previous universe. But whether it has a cause or not, that cause (say atheists) will not be an intentional one, for mental activity is something that has developed very late in the universe's history. As for (ii) and (iii), there is undoubtedly *something* in each case that plays that role, but we should not expect that it is the same thing that explains both – and it is not really a *thing* at all, in the sense of being an object like a tree, or a god. The ultimate source of love, for instance, might be the biological drive to reproduce. The ultimate source of moral knowledge may be within our own psychology.

The details don't matter. The crucial point is that whereas the theist is looking for something that explains (i)–(iii) in a single package, the atheist is not.

Thought of in these terms, does theism have a much lower initial probability than atheism? It isn't at all clear that it does. Of course, once we start filling in the details, going beyond the basic role that God is supposed to play and describing how exactly he plays those roles, then the specificity of the hypothesis goes up, and the initial probability consequently goes down. And the same is true of atheism. Once we go beyond a denial that there is a being that plays the roles in question, and start to fill in the alternative explanations, then the initial probability goes down.

It looks, then, as if theism and atheism start on pretty much the same footing. There should be no presumption of atheism, and indeed no presumption of theism either. The initial position should be an agnostic one, which means that theists and atheists share the burden of proof. Agnosticism is not redundant.

All this is not at all to deny that agnosticism as a considered position must rest on more than the relatively (or, as Dawkins calls it, 'ignominiously') weak point that we cannot prove that God does or does not exist. The fact that we cannot prove that there are trees in a way that will satisfy the philosophical sceptic does not make it at all irrational to continue to believe in trees, and the fact that we cannot prove that Russell's teapot does not exist does not make it at all irrational to continue to believe that there is no such teapot. For most of our beliefs, we can give nothing more than reasonable grounds, and sometimes not even that. So the agnostic will have to show either that we can't even find reasonable grounds that would shift the probabilities one way or the other – towards theism or towards atheism – or that taken together the reasons we give for each side cancel each other out. That would leave us with agnosticism not simply as a starting point, but as a finishing point too.

Chapter 4
Why be agnostic?

The decisive test

It is a mark of a good scientific hypothesis that it is subject to tests whose outcome would confirm or disconfirm it. In some cases, the scientist is in the happy position of making a relatively straightforward observation that confirms the hypothesis decisively. A positive result is a happy occasion indeed. Here are a couple of instances.

In 1639, a young astronomer by the name of Jeremiah Horrocks was studying an account of the movements of the planets by the great astronomer Johannes Kepler. Kepler had predicted that every so often the orbit of Venus would take the planet through a direct line between Earth and the Sun. This transit of the Sun by the planet should, in principle, be observable, though no-one had yet observed it. The last transit was hypothesized to have taken place in 1631. Kepler predicted that Venus would come close to making another transit in 1639, but would not quite do so. Horrocks disagreed: he reasoned that something was not quite right with Kepler's calculations, and that there should be another transit on 24 November of that year. On that day, Horrocks set up his telescope so that it would project an image of the Sun onto a piece of white paper. Conditions were not ideal; in fact, it was a very cloudy day. But by 3.15 pm, the clouds had parted sufficiently for Horrocks to see an unmistakable black dot on the image of the Sun. This was the silhouette of Venus: he had been right.

We move forward to 19 April 1894, when the Scottish chemist William Ramsay was attending a lecture by Lord Rayleigh on the composition of the air. Rayleigh reported that atmospheric nitrogen (isolated by removing by chemical means both oxygen and carbon dioxide from the air) was very slightly denser than nitrogen produced by heating ammonium nitrate. What could explain this? Rayleigh himself thought that there must be an impurity in the nitrogen produced by the chemical method, a lighter gas that was affecting the measurement. Ramsay, however, having recently read of much earlier experiments on nitrogen by Henry Cavendish, suspected that there was a denser gas in the atmospheric nitrogen. He corresponded with Rayleigh, and they agreed to pursue their own hypotheses further. Having, as he hoped, isolated the denser gas in atmospheric nitrogen, Ramsay subjected it to spectroscopic analysis. The spectroscope was then a relatively new piece of equipment in the analytical chemist's armoury. An electric current was passed through a gas (or vapourized substance), producing light that was then split by a prism. The resulting spectrum consisted of a series of lines against a black background. Each element had its own characteristic spectrum. When Ramsay examined the spectrum produced by the gas he had isolated, he found groups of green and red lines not belonging to any known element: conclusive proof that here was a new element. Ramsay and Rayleigh published their results together, and named the new gas *argon* (from the Greek, meaning idle: argon turned out to be almost completely unreactive).

Both Horrocks and Ramsay were able to make relatively simple observations that established the truth of their hypothesis. Horrocks saw the black dot against the Sun's image, and Ramsay saw the unfamiliar lines of light. Both knew at once that they had been right. Is such a test available in the theological sphere? The Old Testament reports just such a test. In the days of the prophet Elijah, many Israelites worshipped a god known as Baal. Elijah, having gathered the priests of Baal on Mount Carmel, proposes the following test. Two piles of wood are to be constructed, in preparation for a burnt offering. One offering is to be made to Baal, another to the Lord, Elijah's God. The offerings are laid, one on each pile, but the wood is not to be lit. The priests are then invited to call upon Baal to send fire to light their pile. They do. Nothing happens. Elijah invites them to call upon Baal more loudly, in case he didn't hear. They do so, and again nothing happens. It is now Elijah's turn. To make it even more stringent a test, he commands water to be poured over the wood, making it wet and harder to light. Then he makes his supplication:

> Hear me, O LORD, hear me, that this people may know that thou art the LORD God, and that thou hast turned their hearts back again.

> Then the fire of the LORD fell, and consumed the burnt sacrifice, and the wood, and the stones, and the dust, and licked up the water that was in the trench.

> And when all the people saw it, they fell on their faces: and they said, The Lord, he is the God.

The result of this test, we would have to agree, was a very significant one, and it spelled bad news for the priests of Baal, who immediately after this incident came to a rather sticky end. But would anyone nowadays suggest such a test for the God hypothesis? And if they carried it out, is it likely that there would be a positive result? I think we'd have to admit that, unlike the prediction of a transit of Venus, or of a hitherto undiscovered element in the atmosphere, no specific test could be devised that would generate a positive result that could be confirmed publicly, and which would satisfy sceptics. What we have instead is a series of observations that, though suggestive, are also very ambiguous in their import. Let us take a look at some of them. I do not propose a systematic study of arguments for and against the God hypothesis, but rather a brief look at a selection of case studies, which illustrate the unavoidable ambiguity of the evidence.

Case study 1: intelligence

There is one striking observation we can make without even using any of our senses – striking, that is, when we stop to think about it – namely, that the world contains intelligence. In other words, there is such a thing as thought, and that thought is able somehow to represent how things actually are in the outside world, speculate on what might be, and initiate action so as to bring about what is desired. Moreover, this representational thought is *conscious*: it brings with it an absolutely mystifying sense of self-awareness (awareness of the thought, that is, if not necessarily also of the thinker).

At one stage in the history of thought, this readily made observation was considered enough to establish that nature had been created by Divine Providence. For how could the random behaviour of atoms give rise to something so complex and purposeful? Faced with a choice between intelligence as the chance result of random motions, and intelligence as the inevitable result of benevolent intervention by God, the attractions of the latter would have seemed irresistible. And, despite the astonishing progress of science, it has not lost all its power today. But, as Dawkins points out, the 'random or designed?' dichotomy is a false one. There is now available an entirely naturalistic explanation of intelligence ('naturalistic' in that it does not appeal to supernatural forces), namely that it is simply one more evolutionary strategy. Intelligence does not simply appear, miraculously, at some particular point in history: it gradually emerges by a series of small steps, a gradual increase in complexity in living systems and their capacity to adapt and survive. A creature lacking intelligence will survive only as long as the capacities with which biological evolution has endowed it fit for its environment. If that environment should change drastically, it has no other resources to fall back on. Intelligence permits a greater degree of flexibility, and this is nowhere more convincingly illustrated than in the case of human beings. The modern human is relatively poorly adapted, biologically speaking, to its environment. But psychological and social evolution has compensated for this by partly insulating the biological being from the ravages of nature: technology and social cooperation provide us with a host of things it would be difficult to obtain by our own unaided efforts: food, clothing, housing, transport.

Natural selection, then, appears to make theism redundant as an explanation of intelligence. But atheists can do more than show that God is not required. They can go on the offensive. The argument from intelligence to God backfires, says Dawkins, because its premise that undesigned intelligence is vastly improbable makes *God* exceedingly improbable. The kind of complexity that intelligence requires only avoids the lowest probability rating if it is either designed by a being who is itself intelligent, or instead the result of gradual changes due to mutation and natural selection over millennia. But God himself is not (according to theism) the result of intelligent design, nor is he the result of natural selection, for he is the creator. We have to conclude that God is highly improbable. And this has consequences for our previous discussion over the assumption of atheism. If the onus is on those who hold a hypothesis that has a low degree of initial improbability to provide convincing evidence for it, and theism is an initially improbable hypothesis, then there must at the outset be a presumption of atheism.

Intelligence seems to be a fickle witness: at first offering apparently overwhelming support for theism, and then (with the aid of a powerful scientific theory) providing instead a devastating argument against it.

But that is not the end of the matter. The kind of intelligence we are familiar with, arising as it apparently does from a very complex brain, is indeed something that has a low initial probability. But need intelligence be like that? The key idea here is that one and the same property can be realized in a variety of ways, some involving less complexity and improbability than others. Take the property of being spherical. As realized by a soap bubble, it is not an improbable property – that is, this particular instance of it is not improbable. The forces within the bubble make this a much more natural shape than a cube, for instance, or a dodecahedron. But now imagine a flock of birds flying overhead forming for a moment a spherical shape. Although the tendency of these birds to fly together makes some kind of shape inevitable (and some formations often give us the strange impression that the flock is a single creature moving through the air), this particular one is highly improbable. Properties, then, can be realized in different ways, and the probability of such a property being realized depends on *how* it is realized. It is not unreasonable to apply this to intelligence. Just how complex and improbable uncaused intelligence would be may depend on how it is realized. And here we are imagining, not simply creatures with a different chemistry to ours, for their brains might well involve the same degree of complexity as ours. Rather, we are imagining something radically different, something that may not involve physical realization at all. Of course, our minds begin to spin at this point, but that should make us all the more cautious about assigning any initial probability to the existence of intelligence.

Aside from this, is it so clear that natural selection shows theism, in this area at least, to be redundant? For, as we said, one of the most remarkable features of intelligence is consciousness. But must intelligence, even of the most sophisticated kind, involve consciousness? We may be prepared to talk of artificial intelligence as a way of describing the truly astounding information-processing capacities of computers. But would we be as prepared to talk of *artificial consciousness*? And this leads to the following thought: if intelligence and consciousness are in principle separable, then perhaps natural selection could have led to a race of incredibly intelligent zombies who used their intelligence to survive in and adapt to changing environments. But they wouldn't be *conscious*. So what is it about natural selection that explains this apparently additional aspect of our mental lives?

That is simply a question. It isn't a decisive blow against atheism. But it should plant another seed of doubt in the mind of anyone who would use the case of intelligence to advance the atheist cause.

Case study 2: life and the laws of nature

A more widespread phenomenon than intelligence is life itself: the world is teeming with it, on land, in water, and in the air. Perhaps it is confined just to this planet, perhaps not. The extent of it does not matter for our purposes. The fact remains that it exists. Should we be surprised by that? In one sense, not at all, since every experience we have had since birth puts us in contact with life (our own, if nothing else's). But in another sense, it *is* surprising, and becomes more so when we look at what had to happen in order for life to emerge out of the soup of organic matter sloshing around billions of years ago.

Here are just some of the conditions that had to be met. First, there had to be the raw ingredients for life, including carbon and hydrogen, since these two elements form the basis of the organic substances of which living things are composed. Second, conditions had to be such that complex proteins were formed out of the simple molecules available, for only such complex substances could form the structures necessary for living bodies. Third, there had to be a source of heat, providing the energy for reactions and a medium in which they could take place, for a completely frozen Earth would also have been a completely unreactive one. Fourth, that source of heat had to be around for long enough, since the emergence and development of life took many billions of years. Fifth, for there to be significant bodies of matter such as the Earth to provide a large enough surface on which life could form, the expansion from the Big Bang had to be neither too fast nor too slow: too fast and matter would not congregate to form larger bodies; too slow and the gravitational forces between material objects would bring about recollapse before galaxies could form. Sixth, for all this to happen, the universe itself had to be relatively stable: it had to be governed by laws of nature, and not completely chaotic.

All this might seem obvious enough, but what is much less obvious is that some of these conditions (the fact that stars have long lives, and that carbon and hydrogen were available in large quantities) depended on what are known as the fundamental constants. These include the precise values of certain forces within atoms. They are constants in that they do not vary from place to place or from time to time, and they are fundamental in that they do not seem to be derived from some more basic property. Less obvious still, and indeed a considerable surprise to scientists reflecting on it, is that the values of each of these fundamental constants had to fall within a very narrow range. Outside that range and life – as we know it – could not have emerged. Assuming that it was completely accidental that the values did fall within the required ranges, the emergence of life was an enormously improbable event. The universe, as it is sometimes put, seems to have been 'fine-tuned' for life. What could explain that?

One explanation is that it really was fine-tuned – by God. God set the values as he did precisely so as to enable life to emerge, which was his ultimate purpose. Without his intervention, life would have been vanishingly improbable. And that, according to some thinkers (including a number of scientists), shifts the probabilities decisively in favour of the God hypothesis.

There are two objections to this way of thinking, however. At first sight, it might seem that there could not possibly be a purely scientific explanation of the fundamental constants, nor of the lawlikeness of the universe. For the constants are precisely *fundamental*, not explicable in terms of something more basic. And scientific explanation presupposes laws. It may derive some laws from other laws, but it cannot explain why it is that there are any. But in fact, there is a purely natural explanation available for the apparent fine-tuning of the universe, and that is that this is just one of many universes, all with their own laws. Perhaps some have no laws whatsoever, and are completely chaotic. But the more universes we suppose there to be, the greater the number of permutations that can be realized, and the more likely that one of these universes will be one where the conditions for life are just right. Naturally, we are going to find ourselves in such a universe. This is the so-called 'multiverse' hypothesis. It is a scientific explanation in so far as it presupposes nothing that could not be described in scientific terms. Could we put the multiverse hypothesis to the test? Not directly. We cannot observe these other universes because they are, in a very special sense, isolated from us. There is no route we or anything else, such as a beam of light, could take from one universe to another, because each universe sits in its own space, and there is no path between them. They are 'parallel worlds', never meeting. This assumption of the spatial separation of universes isn't just a convenient device to stop us wondering why we can't detect them: it is a necessary part of saying that they have their own laws, for laws should govern the whole of space, not just a part of it. But despite not being able to verify directly that they exist, we can use the fact that they would explain what is otherwise a very puzzling fact about this universe, that it supports life, to argue that it is more probable that they exist than not.

So the atheist can offer an alternative explanation of fine-tuning. Which is the more credible hypothesis, God or the multiverse? That depends on your point of view. On the one hand, it might seem less extravagant to posit the existence of just one (admittedly extraordinary) object, namely God, than to posit an enormous number of objects, namely universes. On the other hand, that one object is something very different from anything else we are aware of, whereas the multiverse just contains lots of universes like (or perhaps not so very like) the one we know exists. So we have something of a stalemate between theist and atheist.

A further objection to using fine-tuning to argue for the existence of God – and this is more of a direct attack – is that it is not obvious that God would choose to create a universe which *required* fine-tuning in order for life to emerge. For all we know, he could have created a universe which had the kind of laws which *didn't* require fine-tuning in order for life to emerge. And if he could, it's rather puzzling that he didn't choose this method. So until we know whether or not such a world is possible, we cannot point to fine-tuning as evidence for the existence of God. Unfortunately, on this question, we are just reduced to guesswork: it just isn't clear what would establish the possibility or impossibility of such laws.

Case study 3: the moral conscience

We all know what it is like to have a conscience, and it sometimes gives us a hard time. But what is the source of this thing that prompts us to certain actions, makes us refrain from others, and which generates feelings of guilt or satisfaction? Sometimes, no doubt, they are a response to the perceived approval or disapproval of our actions by other people. But very often we have these feelings *before* being exposed to judgement in this way. Moreover, even contemplating a certain action can be enough to induce these feelings. For John Henry Newman (1801–90), an English cleric who in 1845 left the Church of England to join the Catholic Church, the moral conscience pointed to a divine source:

> These feelings in us are such as to require for their exciting cause an intelligent being: we are not affectionate towards a stone, nor do we feel shame before a horse or a dog; we have no remorse

or compunction on breaking a mere human law: yet, so it is, conscience excites all these painful emotions, confusion, foreboding, self-condemnation; and on the other hand it sheds upon us a deep peace, a sense of security, a resignation, and a hope, which there is no sensible, no earthly object to elicit. 'The wicked flees, when no one pursueth'; Then why does he flee? Whence his terror? Who is it that he sees in solitude, in darkness, in the hidden chambers of his heart? If the cause of these emotions does not belong to this visible world, the Object to which his perception is directed must be Supernatural and Divine.

So even if we are not apparently being observed by any human onlooker when we act as we should or shouldn't, or just contemplate doing so, it feels *as if* we are being observed and judged, and we experience the associated pride or shame. Why would we do this unless there really were such a being observing and judging us, and communicating that judgement to us? For Newman, God is the inescapable conclusion. But let us put the point more modestly and say that the phenomenon of conscience shifts the probabilities somewhat in favour of theism.

But does it? There is an alternative explanation of the source of conscience, and that is that it is the result of both positive and negative conditioning, in which good actions are rewarded and bad ones punished, making us anxious or fearful at the mere thought of performing or avoiding certain actions. We experience approbation and disapprobation when we are at a very young and impressionable age and we internalize these judgements. When we act, it is as if we are being watched by a parent or by someone who has authority over us, because those were exactly the conditions under which we took our first steps towards understanding right and wrong. There is an ineradicable association between act and judgement, so that the performance or contemplation of the former leads inexorably to the expectation of the latter. God, it might be argued, needn't come into it.

That may seem plausible enough, but it cannot be the whole story. The actual experiences we had when young don't seem enough to explain the all-pervasiveness of conscience. Sometimes we did bad things and got away with them; sometimes we did good things and no-one knew. Sometimes we were unjustly punished or unfairly rewarded. Those meting out the judgement may themselves have been morally flawed. And our conscience is stirred by actions we perform as adults that have no counterpart in our childhood experience: how could blind associations generalize in this way? Moreover, this 'conditioned fear response' approach to conscience doesn't explain the peculiarly *moral* sense. We feel embarrassment and shame over many things we do that have no specifically moral content: our lame performance on sports day at school may have led to howls of execration, the shame of which we continue to feel for many years afterwards. But that hardly amounts to a bad conscience. The thought of speaking in public or appearing in certain forms of dress may evoke strong anxiety or embarrassment, but no moral sensations. So what aspect of conditioning explains the moral dimension of our emotions?

We could try supplementing the social conditioning account by one that sees conscience as the legacy of both biological and social evolution over millennia, in which dispositions to certain kinds of behaviour – generally, those that contribute to greater social cohesion – are selected for at the expense of those that are damaging to social groups. Essentially, those who have a hard-wired capacity for moral conscience are, other things being equal, more likely to pass on their genes than those who do not. And societies that develop a collective moral conscience are more likely to survive than those that do not.

So what of Newman's suggestion that our moral feelings intimate the existence of a judge: that the kinds of feelings we have are those we would feel before the gaze of a moral being? We could say that this is just a product of evolution; that these kinds of feelings are more likely to be selected for than those that don't involve the sense of a judge. Or we could say that Newman's reflections on the psychology of conscience are coloured by his own religious beliefs. Because he believes in God, he interprets his feelings in relation to a divine being. Of course, atheists are just as disposed to have moral feelings, but they are unlikely to report those in terms of feeling as if they are being judged by a divine lawmaker.

But there is still something missing from the purely secular account of conscience. Conscience directs us to moral properties of the acts themselves: the act (of murder, theft, and deceit or charity, compassion, and sacrifice) is itself good or evil. That property does not appear to reside in the mind alone. It may be that an action must originate in an evil thought in order to count as bad, but the badness of the action is not the same thing as the badness of the thought. At least, this is how things appear to us, that our moral judgements are intended as picking out moral properties of the acts. This is the (real or apparent) *objectivity* of our moral judgements. Now, if the conscience whose promptings give rise to these judgements is a result of a combination of biological and social selection plus psychological conditioning, where does this sense of objectivity come from? The mechanism is perhaps something like this: we witness, or think about, certain actions, such as deliberate deception, and they induce feelings in us, say of disapproval. This feeling is then somehow projected onto the act itself, resulting in what appears to be a perception of the act's badness.

But this projection – if that is what it is – is very puzzling. It doesn't happen when things induce pain in us, for example. The experience of something may be accompanied by pain – perhaps it is very hot, or sharp, or heavy, or loud. But we don't then project the pain onto the thing that causes it. We may recognize a property in the object as the one that causes the pain, but the painfulness remains firmly fixed to the experience itself. Things are not intrinsically painful: it depends how they are presented to us. Why, then, when actions induce moral feelings in us, does the moral aspect of the experience not just stay fixed to the experience itself, rather than being projected onto the action, so that the action is seen as intrinsically good or bad, however it is presented to us? It isn't at all obvious that there is an explanation of this in terms of natural selection. There is certainly a close connection between moral feelings and feelings of pain and pleasure: guilt is a kind of mental pain, and moral satisfaction a kind of mental pleasure. The intensity of these feelings is enough to explain the role they play in the reinforcement, positive or negative, of certain kinds of behaviour, without the need for them to be taken as detecting objective moral properties in the world. And yet they are taken in this way. Why? Perhaps we have to accept that this is just how things are, that it is simply an accident of nature. But in the light of the God hypothesis, they become more intelligible: such feelings truly are the perception of the goodness or evil which is quite independent of any human beliefs or practices, and which points ultimately to a divine source. This conclusion is not forced on us. It remains an option to think of the apparent objectivity of moral judgements arising from the conscience as an accidental illusion. But it does show that the God hypothesis is not made completely redundant by the theory of natural selection.

Case study 4: the presence of God

It is the night of 2 November 1829, and a young man, Stephen H. Bradley, is lying in bed at home in Connecticut. Earlier that day, he had attended church, and though subjected to a window-rattling and bone-shaking sermon on the terrors of Judgement Day, he had remained curiously unmoved by it. But now, alone with his thoughts in the dark, he feels something strange begin to happen:

> At first, I began to feel my heart beat very quick all on a sudden, which made me at first think that perhaps something is going

to ail me, though I was not alarmed, for I felt no pain. My heart increased in its beating, which soon convinced me that it was the Holy Spirit from the effect it had on me. I began to feel exceedingly happy and humble, and such a sense of unworthiness as I never felt before. I could not very well help speaking out, which I did, and said, Lord, I do not deserve this happiness, or words to that effect, while there was a stream (resembling air in feeling) came into my mouth and heart in a more sensible manner that that of drinking anything, which continued, so near as I could judge, five minutes or more, which appeared to be the cause of such a palpitation of my heart. It took complete possession of my soul, and I am certain that I desired the Lord, while in the midst of it, not to give me any more happiness, for it seemed as if I could not contain what I had got. My heart seemed as if it would burst, but it did not stop until I felt as if I was unutterably full of the love and grace of God. In the mean time while thus exercised, a thought arose in my mind, what can it mean? And all at once, as if to answer it, my memory became exceedingly clear, and it appeared to me just as if the New Testament was placed open before me, eighth chapter of Romans, and as light as if some candle lighted was held for me to read the 26th and 27th verses of that chapter, and I read these words: 'The Spirit helpeth our infirmities with groaning which cannot be uttered.'

The following morning, he rose and read the passage that had come into his mind the previous night 'and every verse seemed almost to speak and confirm it to be truly the Word of God'. When he told his parents of his experiences, it seemed to him as if he were not speaking with his own voice: 'My speech seemed entirely under the control of the Spirit within me.'

What are we to make of this? The sensations and emotions are real enough, but do they convince us that this was truly an encounter with God? This is clearly someone who has already followed a religious path, even if he had deviated from it, and who is sufficiently familiar with the Bible to recognize the passage that had entered his thoughts. What could be more natural for him than to interpret what must indisputably have been an intense experience in terms of ideas that he had lived with for a long time, and which would suggest the possibility of such an experience? If the same thoughts had occurred to someone utterly unfamiliar with this particular form of religion, we would have been far more impressed. Even if we are right to be sceptical of the suggestion that religious experiences provide evidence for the existence of God, however, we should take a critical look at the reasons given for dismissing such experiences as illusory:

1   Not everyone has them.

Part of the suspicion directed at reports of religious experiences arises from the fact that such experiences are far from universal. They do cut across times and cultures, to be sure, but overall they seem to affect only a minority. Of course, the mere fact that a certain kind of experience is rare doesn't make it illusory. Think, for instance, of the very curious phenomenon of 'blind sight', in which totally blind people have apparently been able to detect whether an object is situated to their right or left, although it seemed to them that they were simply guessing. But the relative rarity of perceptions of God should be a puzzle to theists. If God does reveal himself in this way, why is he so selective about it? One answer to this is that to be in contact with God in this way requires willingness on the part of the subject, a desire to be close to God. In this, it may be akin to being hypnotized. Not everyone is susceptible to hypnosis. Those who are may have to give themselves permission to be hypnotized; those who resist do not fall under the spell.

2   There is no sense organ for perceiving God.

A slightly curious objection, perhaps, but certainly worth considering. We perceive things because they impinge on our sense organs. We see a tree, hear the wind rustling its leaves, smell its blossom, and feel its rough bark. But God is not something (we are told) that can be seen, heard, smelled, or touched. How, then, do we perceive him? Presumably through some other organ – but no such organ (that we have been able to discover) exists. Before we jump to the conclusion that God is never perceived, however, we should reflect on the remaining possibilities. The first is that God may contact our minds directly, without the mediation of the body. The second is that, although there is no specific organ devoted to God-detection, we may nevertheless perceive God through perceiving other things by the five senses. An analogy here is time perception. There is no specific time organ, but we still sense such things as the passage of time and the duration of events through what we see and hear (and, to a lesser extent, what we smell and touch).

3   We can artificially induce 'religious' experiences by stimulating the temporal lobes of the brain.

In the 1980s, American neuroscientist Michael Persinger was conducting experiments into the effect of magnetic fields on the brain, especially the temporal lobes. The apparatus he developed has come to be known, perhaps somewhat facetiously, as the 'God helmet'. The helmet contains a number of solenoids which subject selected parts of the brain to weak magnetic fields. Many of those who wore the helmet reported strange sensations, often of another presence in the room with them, and in some cases, the presence was felt to be God. The tempting conclusion to draw from this is that religious experiences are the result of unusual episodes of temporal lobe activity, and some people are more prone to these than others. A further conclusion is that this is *all there is* to religious experiences, and that no supernatural being lies behind them. But that further conclusion is not warranted. Supposing that it is possible to perceive God, there is no reason to think that this would not be through the intermediary of the brain, and perhaps particularly through the temporal lobes. And the fact that some experiences can be artificially induced does not entail that such experiences in general are illusory. Phantom limb pain illustrates the point: amputees may feel pain in a limb such as a leg that has been removed. The pain is real, its apparent location illusory. But that gives us no reason to doubt that we have legs, or to think that that our apparent awareness of them when we get cramp or pins and needles must be mistaken.

4   We have an inbuilt tendency to interpret things as the result of agency.

This is the so-called 'hyperactive agency-detection device'. It's important that animals are able to detect agency when they have evidence for it: those rustling sounds in the bushes may be a predator, that movement in the water may be a fish that would provide useful nutrition, those distinctive sounds may be the call of a potential mate, and so on. Clearly, evolution would favour the development of such a capacity. But it is sometimes triggered in situations when there is no agency. This doesn't put us at a disadvantage, since it is clearly better, from the viewpoint both of survival in the wild, and, at a more advanced level, to the well-functioning of a social group, to detect agency that isn't there than to fail to detect agency that is. Hyperactivity is better than hypoactivity in this context. Could religious experiences, and religious belief in general, just be the over-enthusiastic promptings of the agency-detection device? Perhaps we are hard-wired to see agency in the workings of the cosmos when there is none. The reply to this is the same as to the previous objection: that a sensory or information-processing system can occasionally misfire is no reason to mistrust it, but rather to treat it with some caution.

5   Religious experiences do not appear to be the source of completely new ideas or concepts to those who have them; they are just interpreted in the light of beliefs already held or entertained.

That objection is certainly confirmed by the case of Stephen H. Bradley's account of his experience, above. But for the religious beliefs or ideas already in the mind of the subject, would the experiences in question have been counted as anything to do with God in the first place? That seems doubtful, although we cannot rule it out. But then, this is not peculiar to religious beliefs. It is an example of a wider phenomenon: our observations of the world and ourselves, however apparently simple and direct, are coloured by the ideas, assumptions, and theories we have. We can see a tree just by virtue of standing in front of it in good lighting conditions with our eyes open and looking in the right direction. But we won't see it *as* a tree unless we already possess the concept of a tree, built up gradually from encounters with trees and references to them. Ambiguous drawings can be seen first as one thing, and then as another: is that a black candlestick or two white faces? Are we above the staircase looking down, or below the staircase looking up? Sometimes the interpretative mechanisms are in-built rather than acquired. Sometimes a shift in the retinal image of an object will make us see the object as moving, sometimes not, depending on what other information is coming into the brain. If the retinal image is shifting because we are turning our head, for example, we won't typically see motion. At a much higher level of sophistication, the kinds of observations that are held to confirm or disconfirm scientific theories will themselves have quite a bit of science built into them. 'The liquid turned a milky colour' may not be sufficient to confirm a hypothesis, whereas a more theory-laden report of the same observation ('A precipitate of calcium carbonate was produced') may well be. Removing all scientific content from the reports we give of experiments and observations would make the testing of scientific theory practically impossible. But that is not taken as undermining the claims of science to reveal something of the nature of reality.

Each one of these objections to using reports of religious experience to support the God hypothesis should make us cautious of accepting those reports at face value. But we can't take them as completely discrediting those reports unless we are prepared to entertain an uncomfortable degree of scepticism about our non-religious beliefs.

Case study 5: the absence of God

If some people feel the presence of God, many others are struck by his absence. It is not just that they see nothing in nature and human existence that suggests divine authorship: they see things that positively tell against it. There is no shortage of cases where a benevolent God could intervene to good effect, and relieve the intense suffering that is the result of famine, floods, disease, earthquakes, war, terrorism, political instability, religious intolerance... and yet he does not. Why? This is probably the hardest objection the theist has to answer. The undeniable fact of suffering and our failure to lead the kind of lives that we suppose God would wish us to lead undermine the God hypothesis, argues the atheist, since the existence of God should make it less rather than more probable that suffering, evil, and imperfection should be as widespread and devastating as they clearly are. The probability of that hypothesis being true thus goes down in the light of the evidence. In contrast, the hypothesis that the world as we know it is a product, not of deliberate agency, but blind and morally indifferent forces, and human nature the result of a fight for survival through millennia of evolution, would make it very likely that suffering and evil would be rife. The probability of that hypothesis thus goes up in the light of the evidence.

That the world looks very much as if it had not been guided by God, that there is a remarkable lack of evidence of his hand at work, is admitted by no less committed a believer than Cardinal Newman. No one has put it more clearly or poignantly:

> To consider the world in its length and breadth, its various history, the many races of men, their starts, their fortunes, their mutual alienation, their conflicts; and then their ways, habits, governments, forms of worship; their enterprises, their aimless

courses, their random achievements and acquirements, the impotent conclusion of long-standing facts, the tokens so faint and broken of a superintending design, the blind evolution of what turn out to be great powers or truths, the progress of things, as if from unreasoning elements, not towards final causes, the greatness and littleness of man, his far-reaching aims, his short duration, the curtain hung over his futurity, the disappointments of life, the defeat of good, the success of evil, physical pain, mental anguish, the prevalence and intensity of sin ... all this is a vision to dizzy and appal; and inflicts upon the mind the sense of a profound mystery, which is absolutely beyond human solution.

Though declaring it beyond solution, Newman nevertheless draws an uncompromising inference: 'either there is no Creator, or this living society of men is in a true sense discarded from his presence'. The first of these is for him unthinkable, since his own conscience makes him as certain of God's existence as he is of his own. That leaves us with the second, scarcely less bleak, conclusion: God is, to all appearances, absent because he has withdrawn, leaving us to our own devices.

As an explanation, this is not entirely satisfactory. If God has withdrawn, why did he do so? Presumably, because the human race went off the rails rather badly. But why did they do so? If the current parlous state of humanity is due to the absence of God's guiding hand, why, when it was active, did that hand not prevent corruption before it took hold? And here is another concern. At what point did God withdraw? Not, surely, before the creation of the world itself. Yet the world appears to have been in the hands of blind forces from the beginning. If the purpose of existence was, ultimately, the creation of conscious life which would be capable of love, goodness, and understanding, why take this extraordinarily indirect and wasteful route to it? Why did it require so many false starts, so much destruction, such a long period of inanimacy? And why, when it did appear, was it concentrated in so small a part of a vast and largely empty universe? The problem for theists, then, is not simply why there is so much suffering, though that is a hard problem enough: it is also why God would have chosen this particular way of realizing his ends – the *problem of superfluity*, we might call it.

On the specific question of suffering, some theists frankly admit that they do not know why God permits such things, but trust that he has a reason. Others offer the consideration that suffering as a result of human evil is an inevitable consequence of the gift of free will. A truly loving God would have no interest in creating automata that invariably chose the right course of action. Instead, he made us autonomous, and that means that we sometimes choose wrongly. To intervene each time a wrong decision was taken, in order to nullify any evil consequences, would frustrate that freedom. It would no longer matter what we chose. This, of course, fails to explain the suffering brought about by natural disasters. Here, it might be suggested that suffering, whether as a result of natural disaster or human evil, is necessary for our becoming truly moral beings with compassion for others and a capacity to put their interests before our own.

Does this 'character-building' solution to the problem of suffering, if that does not seem too facetious a name for it, also offer an answer to the problem of superfluity? The idea might be this. In so far as the world and its inhabitants are the product of blind (although not random) forces, it is up to us to shape them as we see fit. What good there is must come from us. Any indication that it will come from elsewhere might lead us into dangerous passivity. It is as if (so the story goes) God intends us to look at the world and feel alone, for only then will we realize that it is up to us to make heaven on Earth.

How plausible a story is that? Plausible enough to make us hesitate before taking the apparent absence of God as a mark in favour of atheism.

What this all-too-brief survey of five pieces of evidence is intended to show is just how ambiguous that evidence is. Whenever we find a reason for thinking that the evidence in question shifts the probabilities one way, towards theism or towards atheism, there is a further consideration that pulls in the opposite direction. The case for agnosticism, then, is this: there is no firm basis on which we can judge atheism to have a greater intrinsic probability than theism. They begin the race on exactly the same line, neither having a head start. And the evidence that we subsequently examine is sufficiently ambiguous that we cannot at any later point decide that one hypothesis has a greater overall probability than the other.

The atheist, however, has a further move to make. 'Is agnosticism not self-defeating?' he asks. 'For surely a benevolent God would not make it so hard to work out, from the evidence in front of us, that he exists. Why not give his creation the gift of certainty rather than the burden of doubt? The very grounds for agnosticism therefore make atheism more likely, and so we should rationally choose atheism rather than remain completely agnostic.' But if the theist has a satisfactory response to the problem of God's apparent absence, then the agnostic has an answer to this latest objection from the atheist. The fact that we cannot rid ourselves of doubt and uncertainty does not make theism less likely. It may be part of God's plan that we should fashion ourselves, that we should become autonomous beings. That uncertainty is what makes us what we are, and we are the greater for it. It may be, as Thomas More says in Robert Bolt's play *A Man For All Seasons*, that 'Man he made to serve him wittily, in the tangle of his mind.'

Chapter 5
Does agnosticism rest on a mistake?

Three assumptions

To be an agnostic is to assume certain things about belief in God, and although those assumptions might seem at first glance entirely reasonable, the possibility remains that they are, in fact, false, or at least subject to serious objections. So we should bring those assumptions out into the open. Are they defensible?

Let's pick out four vital assumptions about the God hypothesis:

(i) it is either true or false;
(ii) it is to be understood literally;
(iii) belief in its truth is only rational if based on reasons that don't just assume that God exists;
(iv) those reasons must appeal to sufficient evidence for the hypothesis.

That the first of these is an assumption of agnosticism is obvious enough: if there is something you don't know, then there is something that is true (e.g. that God exists, or that he doesn't exist) but you don't know that it's true. It makes no sense to say that you don't know whether 'doorknob infiltrating as if u-turn' is true, because 'doorknob infiltrating as if u-turn' isn't something that is capable of being true or false. Similar remarks apply to more meaningful phrases like 'let's all keep quite calm'.

What of the second? The atheist/theist debate is at its sharpest when the God hypothesis is interpreted literally, and indeed most atheists interpret it this way. It is the question whether there really exists a transcendent being responsible for the cosmos which atheists answer in the negative, and it is precisely this question that agnostics say can't be answered. As for the third, it seems only fair not to permit arguments for God's existence that beg the question, if we would apply this principle to other debates. What would a physicist make of an argument for black holes that, at some point, just helped itself to the assumption that there were such things? And as for the fourth, it is precisely because agnostics think that the evidence we have for God is doubtful that they are agnostic. If they thought it adequate, they would be theists.

So apparently anodyne are these assumptions that they often escape notice. But they have been challenged.

Revolution in Vienna

In 1929, a pamphlet entitled *The Scientific Conception of the World* was published in Vienna. Its authors were a group of philosophers led by Moritz Schlick, who was professor of the History and Philosophy of the Inductive Sciences at the university. On the title page of the pamphlet this group described themselves as 'the Vienna Circle', and this was their manifesto. It proposed principles by which the meaningfulness (or otherwise) and justification of certain assertions about the world could be assessed. The Circle had begun as a discussion group, originally entitled the 'Ernst Mach Society', named after Schlick's predecessor but one. Its activities were, however, brought to an end soon after the National Socialist, or Nazi, party came to power in Germany in 1933. As Austria came increasingly under Nazi domination, a number of the Circle left the country. Schlick himself was assassinated in 1936 by a student sympathetic to the Nazi cause.

The philosophical outlook that sprang from the writings of the Circle became known as *logical positivism*, and it was promoted in the English-speaking world by the young A. J. Ayer in 1936. Ayer, an Oxford philosopher, had persuaded the publisher Victor Gollancz to give him a contract to write a book on the new philosophy. The result was the polemical *Language, Truth and Logic*, still regarded as the classic statement of a view of meaning known as the criterion, or principle, of verifiability. According to this principle, a sentence (more precisely, a declarative sentence, such as 'the sun is shining', or 'the leaves are falling', rather than a question, wish, or request) is meaningful only to the extent that there are specifiable ways by which we could go about testing it, whose outcome would enable us to determine whether it was true or false. *Can it be verified* (by observation, experiment, or mathematical or logical proof) is the question we have to ask, and if the answer to that question is 'no: nothing we can do would help us to find out whether it is true or false', then the sentence, considered as an assertion, lacks meaning altogether. This view of meaning is clearly inspired by science: scientific inquiry and its methods are here being used as the model to which language should conform.

The criterion of verifiability may not seem particularly surprising, and certainly not revolutionary, but it brought about what we might describe without hyperbole as an intellectual revolution. How? Because, according to the people who subscribed to it, it exposed as *meaningless* whole areas of discourse, and forced a reassessment of the true meaning of other areas. Ayer used it, for instance, to dismiss many of the traditional debates of metaphysics, that part of philosophy that is concerned with the ultimate nature of reality. Metaphysical theories purport to describe the world – they aren't just definitions of terms like 'existence', 'cause', and so on. But, being

8. The man who brought logical positivism to the English-speaking world: A. J. Ayer

metaphysical rather than scientific, they go beyond anything that could be established by observation. So, concludes Ayer, they are meaningless. In this, he was (as he acknowledged) anticipated two centuries earlier by David Hume. But Ayer also applied the criterion to ethical discourse – talk of right and wrong – not to dismiss it as meaningless, for ethical talk is something we can hardly do without, but to show that it was not in the business of stating truths at all. Later, Karl Popper, who was critical of logical positivism, appealed to the related criterion of *falsifiability* to argue that Freudian psychoanalytic theory was devoid of content.

One of the most far-reaching effects of the new philosophy was on attitudes towards theological discourse. For statements about God are supposed to be about the world, rather than merely definitional, and yet they also transcend any possible human experience. Indeed, theists may point out that the transcendental nature of God means that theism cannot readily be falsified or verified as a scientific hypothesis. This way of defending theism, however, is likely to backfire. Ayer's own view of the matter is put in uncompromising terms towards the end of *Language, Truth and Logic*:

> ...if 'god' is a metaphysical term, then it cannot even be probable that a god exists. For to say that 'God exists' is to make a metaphysical utterance which cannot be either true or false...

> It is important not to confuse this view of religious assertions with the view that is adopted by atheists or agnostics. For it is characteristic of an agnostic to hold that the existence of a god is a possibility in which there is no good reason either to believe or disbelieve; and it is characteristic of an atheist to hold that it is at least probable that no god exists. And our view that all utterances about the nature of God are nonsensical, so far from being identical with, or even lending support to, either of these familiar contentions, is actually incompatible with them.

Even so, if everyone were to agree that theism is *either* false *or* meaningless, the practising atheist will probably not mind which, and be content to leave it to philosophers to argue the toss. The point is that theism seems definitely ruled out. In addition, it looks as if there is an argument here to the effect that agnosticism is actually self-defeating. For agnosticism is based on the reflection that what evidence we have does not unambiguously favour either theism or atheism. But if it turns out that no *possible* evidence would help us decide, then theism is unverifiable and so, according to the verifiability criterion, meaningless. And if it is meaningless, then it cannot be said that we do not know whether it is true or false. So the grounds for agnosticism threaten to make it redundant.

However, we shouldn't feel forced by the criterion of verifiability to dismiss theism as meaningless. First, it seems reasonable to ask whether the criterion applies to itself: is there any way of verifying that the principle is true? If not, then, by its own lights, it seems that it must dismiss itself as meaningless. So let us say we try to verify it by looking at cases of sentences we would be inclined (prior to applying any principle) to think of as meaningful. As long as we stick to ordinary statements like 'there is an unopened tin of tomatoes in the left-hand cupboard', the criterion is safe: statements like that clearly satisfy it. But what if we encounter more controversial statements such as 'there is a transcendent creator'? Do we say, since the criterion does not apply to it, this statement is not meaningful after all? Or do we say, since this sentence is meaningful, there must be something wrong with the criterion? If we are in the business of testing the criterion, rather than just assuming its truth, the latter response will remain a possibility.

In any case, it is arguably only a rather strong form of the criterion that threatens traditional, unreconstructed theism. If we are required to come up with a conclusive test for a statement's truth before it is allowed to be meaningful, then not just theism but most of science will be under threat. Science has progressed by the replacement of discredited theories by ones that, in their turn, are discredited. Very little is *conclusively* established. Even a statement as apparently basic and secure as 'there are electrons' is not immune to the vicissitudes of scientific enquiry. A more modest, and therefore more defensible, verificationist principle would require only that meaningful statements about the world would, if true, have consequences for what we could in principle observe. And we can form plenty of hypotheses about God that would have such consequences, such as that he speaks to us through our moral conscience. Theism is not *irrelevant* to what we observe around us, and within ourselves. If it were, no-one would care about it. The difficulty, as the agnostic recognizes, is that these observational consequences are compatible with a quite different hypothesis, the atheistic one.

But now perhaps the principle has been weakened too much. Surely it is reasonable to expect that the difference between theism and atheism should show up *somewhere* in the range of possible experience. So, on a middle-strength version of the verifiability principle, a statement is meaningful to the extent that we can imagine a possible experience or observation that would shift the probabilities in favour of taking that statement to be true (or indeed false). Now if the agnostic argues that no observation will shift the probabilities, either for or against the God hypothesis, then it looks as if the hypothesis comes out meaningless on this criterion of meaning, and so agnosticism is completely redundant.

This is where the difference between different strengths of agnosticism comes into play. If the agnostic is saying merely that no observation made thus far shifts the probabilities, but there are possible observations that would, then there is nothing to fear from the criterion. If the position is a stronger one, that *no possible observation* could shift the probabilities – the issue is in principle undecidable – then there is a challenge here. One way of meeting it would be to say that the God hypothesis remains meaningful because it can be explained by means of statements of the kind that appear in other contexts, contexts in which it is clear how we would set about testing those statements for truth.

The new theologians

Ayer's criterion only applies, of course, to sentences that are used, or intended, as assertions. It does not apply to questions ('would you like some more tea?') or commands ('shut that door!') or wishes ('oh to be in Virginia in the spring!') or expressions of emotion ('aaarrrggghhhh!!!') or statements in fiction ('One sunny day, Alfred Smallwood was returning home from visiting his grandmother when, turning a corner of the street, he stepped into the fourth dimension.') For none of these is intended as expressing a truth or a falsehood. That is why moral utterances escape verificationist censure: for Ayer, they are not assertions, but expressions of feeling, of approval or disgust. As verificationists recognized, utterances that would be nonsense *as assertions* can nevertheless have some kind of meaning.

The possibility remains, therefore, that theological sentences too belong to one or more of these categories: that they are expressive of emotions, or wishes, or else are fictional, used to construct a game of make-believe. If so, then the verifiability criterion cannot touch them. The idea could be expressed like this. Talk 'about God' is *not* a matter of making *assertions* about some transcendent reality, a world that is somehow beyond the world of ordinary experience. To say that God exists is not to say something that is either true or false. It is rather expressive of a commitment to certain values, a desire to live a certain kind of life, a willingness to view things from a certain perspective. The meaning of religious utterance can then be given in terms of the dispositions and behaviour which go with it. This conception of religion has been associated with the Austrian philosopher Ludwig Wittgenstein (1889–1951), who spent much of his professional career at Cambridge, and whose often enigmatic and aphoristic writings (largely in the form of notebooks he didn't intend for publication) have had a profound influence on a very extensive range of philosophical debates. Whether or not Wittgenstein himself quite intended this interpretation, it is a view of religious discourse that has explicitly been defended by those who wished to reconcile theology with logical positivism.

Why didn't Ayer consider this possibility? Perhaps because he felt that, whereas moral statements are indispensable, theological ones are not.

There is another possibility: although the sentences of theology or religion are indeed assertions, they are in *code*. They do not say what they appear to say. They *appear* to be about a transcendent being, the all-knowing, all-powerful creator of the world. What they are actually about is something quite different: us, our ideals and aspirations, our capacity for selfless love, and so on. Once decoded, religious statements may be verified by a study of our psychology.

For a significant part of the 20th century, religious language was reinterpreted or reconstructed in a variety of ways by both philosophers and theologians, though not primarily as a response to the demands of verificationism. For example, the German theologians Rudolf Bultmann (1884–1976) and Paul Tillich (1886–1965) offered 'demythologized' interpretations of Christian scripture and doctrine, in which language about the transcendent is translated into truths about the human response to the world, to others, and to the moral conscience. Their ideas were taken up in England by John Robinson (1919–83), who, as bishop of Woolwich, caused a sensation when in 1963 he published *Honest to God*. The book was Robinson's attempt to present to the general public his sympathetic reflections on Tillich's view of God as the ground of being. OUR IMAGE OF GOD MUST GO was the incendiary headline to an article written by Robinson for the *Observer* two days before the book's publication. The image that had to go was that of a divine person, dispensing justice and occasional rewards rather like, in Robinson's simile, some distant aunt. Instead, God was to be seen not as a person at all, but the personal ground of being, the ultimate reality, what is of fundamental significance in our lives. On a 'non-metaphysical' reading of this view, 'God' is just a name for human impulses and ideals, something entirely within us, but somehow projected outwards.

Whatever the precise details of these approaches to religious language – whether such language is represented as metaphorical, or expressive, or fictional (and it would be unwise to assume that the new theologians were all saying the same thing) – it looks very much as though from this perspective, the God hypothesis isn't a hypothesis at all. It isn't, that is, intended as a theory about the origin of the world, and the source and object of our moral and spiritual impulses. We can group these ideas together under the name *religious non-realism* ('realism' being the view that religion is about a transcendent reality). And it also looks as if, once it is made absolutely explicit what the religious non-realists are committing themselves to, there is very little that the atheist could not also commit to, apart from the continued use of theological language. Small wonder that many believers felt that the bishop, and those thinkers who had inspired him, were really just disguised atheists themselves.

Setting aside the very pertinent question of just what it is, apart from a form of words, that separates the religious non-realist from the atheist, if theism is reconstructed in these kinds of ways, isn't agnosticism just inappropriate? For there is no longer a reason to think that whatever is conveyed by 'God exists' is something we wouldn't be able to establish as true (or false), just by looking at ourselves and our fellow human beings. Well, perhaps we shouldn't be agnostic about aspects of our own nature – or perhaps we should. But that doesn't displace agnosticism as it has been presented in the pages of this book, namely an uncertainty as to whether there is, or is not, a being that is quite independent of any human thought or activity, a being that would, if we understood its nature, provide a single unified explanation of why the world exists, what we are doing in it, and how we should live. That issue will not go away, even if every theologian decided to ignore it.

It may not have 'gone away', responds the non-realist, in the sense that the issue *could* still be debated, but it is religiously frivolous. What matters is our human response to the human condition, not whether there really exists some parent figure who will make everything come right, however we botch things. Preoccupation with such a figure may be excusable in a child, but once we reach maturity it should have no place in our thinking, for it diverts us from the realization that it is *we* who must put things right, *we* who must fashion the world according to the most exalted ideals.

Once again, the atheist will agree with these words, but will find it all the more puzzling that, having reached this insight, the non-realist still finds a place for traditional religious language and imagery. If belief in a transcendent being stops us from becoming fully autonomous, responsible adults, then won't we be similarly hindered by talk of such a being (even if, at some level, we recognize that it is just an image or a metaphor?). And yet, the non-realist seems to suggest that continuing to engage in such talk actually helps us become the people we ought to be. How can this be? We'll come back to this issue later. Meanwhile, the point remains that the non-realist cannot be indifferent to traditional agnosticism. For it is precisely the agnostic realization that the debate over the God hypothesis has not been resolved, and perhaps cannot be resolved, that is one of the motivating forces behind the new theology.

The structure of belief

> I was, at that time, in Germany, whither the wars, which have not yet finished there, had called me, and as I was returning from the coronation of the Emperor to join the army, the onset of winter held me up in quarters in which, finding no company to distract me, and having, fortunately, no cares or passions to disturb me, I spent the whole day shut up in a room heated by an enclosed stove, where I had complete leisure to meditate on my own thoughts.

So the man who has been called the father of modern philosophy, René Descartes (1596–1650), begins his account of a series of reflections that resulted in a complete restructuring of thought. Descartes' guiding question was this: how could human knowledge attain absolute certainty? He was much struck by the power of mathematics to reach, by a series of secure steps, a conclusion based only on self-evident truths. If only something like mathematical proof were available when it came to knowledge of oneself and of the world! Might this be possible? The difficulty is that so much of our belief about the world, unlike mathematical belief, comes from the senses, which are capable of deceiving us. Descartes started with the radical thought that he needed to clear away every belief that he was capable of doubting, leaving only those beliefs which were absolutely self-evident. Thus he arrived at the famous *Cogito ergo sum*: 'I think therefore I am.' Whatever I can be deluded about, I cannot possibly be deluded when I reflect that I am thinking, for without thought (or a thinker to think those thoughts) there can be no delusion! From this at once momentous and severely limited thought, Descartes gradually builds up his system of knowledge, which depends crucially on his demonstration of God's existence.

What Descartes offers us is a picture of knowledge as something that is built on *foundations*: beliefs that are themselves so evidently true that they do not need to be inferred from any other belief. Upon these beliefs, we build further beliefs that depend on the self-evident beliefs. Upon that second layer of belief, we build yet more, and so on. The result can be compared to a pyramid, in which each layer of stone except the very bottom one rests upon a lower layer. The firmness of the whole structure depends on the firmness of the foundation.

If this is the right way to picture knowledge, what kind of belief should we place at the bottom of this structure? Descartes is clear about this: only those beliefs that we perceive by the clear light of reason to be self-evident. But that is not the only answer we might give. We might prefer the bottom layer to be composed of ordinary sensory beliefs ('the air feels warm, there is not a cloud in the sky, a bird is singing overhead', and so on). But, whatever else we might put in this bottom layer, is this the place to put beliefs about

God? One of the assumptions characteristic of the agnostic attitude is that beliefs about God should *not* be treated as basic in this sense. Rather, they should be inferred from, or justified on the basis of other, more fundamental beliefs, beliefs that aren't themselves explicitly about God. Examples of those more fundamental beliefs might include the regularity of the universe, the existence of intelligence, our capacity to love, and so on. The assumption that beliefs about God should not be treated as basic would until relatively recently have been shared by many on both sides of the theism/atheism debate. But about thirty years ago, philosophers started to question that assumption. Why shouldn't belief in God be treated as something that could properly belong in the *foundation* of someone's system of belief? God beliefs could then be beliefs in terms of which other beliefs could be justified. It would then be no objection to religious belief that other beliefs did not adequately support it. It would not need such support. Rather, it would provide support for other beliefs.

Of course, this isn't a licence to put just any old belief at the foundation of one's system. Perhaps the belief that every one of his thoughts and actions is being controlled by Venusians is basic for Stanley: it is a belief that informs every one of his other beliefs. But Stanley is not reasonable. That belief just shouldn't be basic: it needs quite a lot of quite sophisticated justification. A basic belief still has to be grounded in something. It cannot be something that is just picked at random and then, through a massive failure of its unfortunate victim to engage in self-criticism, becomes more deeply embedded in his outlook. So those who say that belief in God is *properly* basic, can appropriately be at the foundation of one's system of thought, assert that such belief is grounded: it is not *inferred* from experience, but there is some aspect of experience which both causes it and guarantees its truth. The comparison here is with ordinary perceptual belief. I believe that there is a tree in front of me, not because I infer the existence of the tree from some other, more basic belief. I just find myself, as a result of an experience (that isn't itself a belief, but a

God? One of the assumptions characteristic of the agnostic attitude is that beliefs about God should *not* be treated as basic in this sense. Rather, they should be inferred from, or justified on the basis of other, more fundamental beliefs, beliefs that aren't themselves explicitly about God. Examples of those more fundamental beliefs might include the regularity of the universe, the existence of intelligence, our capacity to love, and so on. The assumption that beliefs about God should not be treated as basic would until relatively recently have been shared by many on both sides of the theism/atheism debate. But about thirty years ago, philosophers started to question that assumption. Why shouldn't belief in God be treated as something that could properly belong in the *foundation* of someone's system of belief? God beliefs could then be beliefs in terms of which other beliefs could be justified. It would then be no objection to religious belief that other beliefs did not adequately support it. It would not need such support. Rather, it would provide support for other beliefs.

state), having the belief that there is a tree in front of me. That there really is a tree in front of me both causes my belief and makes it true, and in consequence my belief is grounded and so justified.

Does this analogy between religious belief and perceptual belief stand up? Attractive though it is, it's vulnerable to the following objection. In the case of ordinary sensory perception, the best explanation for our beliefs is that they are the result of situations which mirror those beliefs more or less precisely. Natural selection will favour those organisms that successfully perceive relevant features of their environment (food, predator, mate, obstacle, hazard, hiding place, etc.). Moreover, having studied the way in which the senses work, their structure and physiology, we can see just how they manage to be sensitive to features of the environment. We are not in anything like the same position with regard to religious experience. It may be that those experiences do indeed reflect a divine origin. But there are other, entirely plausible explanations of those experiences that are not divine at all. So there is no presumption in favour of those experiences accurately reflecting what they seem to indicate. And as long as there is that uncertainty, God beliefs cannot be regarded as properly belonging to the foundational level of any system of rational belief.

It might be objected that similar scruples apply to ordinary sensory experience. There are, surely, other explanations of our experiences on which they turn out to be systematically illusory. Can we be sure that those hypotheses are not the correct ones? If not, are sensory beliefs properly regarded as basic, fit to be put at the foundation of our belief system? Admittedly, there are these other hypotheses, and perhaps we cannot prove them false. But the problem is that they are totally *outré*, involving, for example, the suggestion that our brains are being artificially stimulated in a laboratory so as to induce a series of coherent but wholly illusory experiences. Such a hypothesis, in all its bizarre detail, is surely less probable than that our sensory experiences, most of the time, reflect things pretty much as they are. In contrast, there is nothing *outré* about the suggestion that there is no God, but a combination of an overactive agency-detecting device, a vivid imagination, and cultural influences, all combine to give rise to experiences that are interpreted as religious ones.

William James: passion and credulity

One evening in 1896 there took place a meeting of the combined philosophical clubs of Brown and Yale universities. The meeting was addressed by the great Harvard philosopher and psychologist William James (1842–1910). If Descartes was the father of modern philosophy, then James certainly has some claim to be the father of modern psychology. He occupied one of the very first established chairs in the subject, at Harvard between 1889 and 1897, when he was appointed professor of philosophy, a post he held until 1907. His talk that evening was entitled 'The Will to Believe', which he presented as a justification of religious faith. That may seem a very ambitious theme, but James had a particular target in mind: the agnostic principle. In fact, he had a particularly uncompromising statement of that principle in his sights. It was due to the mathematician William Kingdom Clifford, who had written, in his essay 'The Ethics of Belief', 'it is wrong always, everywhere, and for anyone, to believe anything upon insufficient evidence'. James set about defending religious belief indirectly, by attacking this principle.

How many of our beliefs actually meet the high standards imposed by Clifford's principle? Very few, suggests James:

> Here, in this room, we all of us believe in molecules and the
> conservation of energy, in democracy and necessary progress, in
> Protestant Christianity and the duty of fighting for 'the doctrine of
> the immortal Monroe,' all for no reasons worthy of the name.

9. **Mathematician William Kingdom Clifford: best known for his uncompromising statement of the agnostic principle**

But how can we believe, and not be at fault, if we do not have sufficient evidence? We may believe because of what others have told us: 'Our faith is faith in some one else's faith.' Many of our scientific beliefs are ones we would be stumped to justify through our own resources, but we put our trust in those whom we suppose to be in a better position to assess them. But we are also influenced by what James calls 'our passional nature'. Where reason stops short of belief, our emotions and desires press us on. Rose believes that Jack likes her, even though the objective evidence for that is as yet not entirely conclusive (he could always be dissembling), and is motivated to believe this by her own liking for him. And, fortunately, it is Jack's perception of Rose's liking for him that confirms his liking for her. Here, belief to some extent anticipates the very thing that vindicates it. Can it on that score be criticized?

Neither of these plausible observations by themselves do much to advance the case for religious faith. First, if we believe in God because others do, our trust may be misplaced. Are they in a better position to know than us? Perhaps they have thought about it for longer, and more deeply, and come to the conclusion that there is a God. Or perhaps they have had an experience in the light of which disbelief is not an option. But there will always be room for doubt here: their reasons may not stand up to public scrutiny. Second, in the case of Rose and Jack, Rose's belief that Jack likes her is part of the cause of Jack's actually liking her: a belief can in this case contribute to bringing about the very conditions that make it true. But that simply doesn't apply in the case of belief in God: how can belief help to bring it about that God actually exists? God is not Tinkerbell, who is kept alive by professions of belief in fairies.

James has another argument, however. When it comes to belief, there are two policies we could follow. The first, which is Clifford's own professed policy, is to avoid error *at all costs*. The second is to pursue truth. Now we might hope to pursue both of these, to avoid error *and* to pursue truth. But in practice, we have to give one priority over the other, because they pull in different directions. If our overriding concern is to avoid being fooled, then we will demand the most rigorous tests before we accept something as true. But the consequence is that we will sometimes fail to perceive the truth: there are true beliefs we might have had that we now have to forgo. In contrast, if our overriding concern is not to miss any truth that is out there, or at least not the most important ones, then we will have to be less demanding in our tests, or put the bar to acceptance rather lower. The cost is that we will sometimes be led into error. Now, says James, the choice between these two policies is itself a passional one: it is our emotions that draw us towards one rather than another: Clifford clearly has a horror of being duped. James, in contrast, is much less concerned about being duped (we are flawed human beings, after all, and will end up occasionally being deceived, however scrupulous we are) than he is about missing out on some momentous truth.

The policy that James is urging on us is no licence to uncritical credulity: we should not rush to adopt just any exciting idea that comes our way: we should still continue to exercise our critical faculties. Nor should we seek to form a view on everything under the sun. Some matters are either too trivial (are there exactly 34,786 leaves on this tree?) or else wouldn't make a difference to us in particular, though they might make a difference to others (how many ships left with Columbus on his voyage to the New World?). Here we can safely wait until we have conclusive evidence before committing ourselves, if we have any interest in the matter. But some matters are so momentous that we may have to risk committing ourselves before all the evidence is in, as we might otherwise wait forever. In addition, some choices between competing beliefs are *forced*, to use James's word. That is, there is no third possibility. A choice between believing that it will rain this afternoon and believing that it will snow is not forced on us, because the possibility remains that it will neither rain nor snow. So where we have choices that are neither forced nor momentous, agnosticism may be a very sensible policy. But choosing between theism and atheism is both forced (either God exists or he doesn't) and momentous.

10. A psychologist who wrote like a novelist: the brilliantly rhetorical
William James

This third argument of James's is a strong one, and it can be made stronger: suppose we recast each policy ('pursue truth!', 'avoid error!') as an assertion. The injunction to avoid error at all costs becomes the judgement that it is better, where there is a conflict between the two policies, to adopt the 'avoid error' policy at the expense of the 'pursue truth' one. How do we know this to be true? The 'avoid error' policy will force us to confess that we do not know it to be true. In contrast, the 'pursue truth' policy will present a much less formidable obstacle to our accepting that it is better to pursue truth than avoid falsehood. It looks, then, as if Clifford's agnostic principle is in trouble.

Note, however, that Clifford's principle does not tell us what counts as 'sufficient' evidence. Is it evidence so overwhelming that it can leave no room for doubt? This is evidently what James takes it to mean. Or is it evidence that is enough to push the probabilities one way rather than the other, so that accepting a hypothesis looks more justified than accepting its denial? That, surely, is consistent with James's policy of pursuing truth while not suspending one's critical faculties. The test case will be where the probabilities seem evenly matched. Since reason cannot decide the truth of the matter, why should our feelings not then make the final decision? Agnosticism may be rational, but, suggests James, it is not emotionally sustainable. How should the agnostic respond to this challenge? We have now moved from purely theoretical considerations to more practical ones, and that is the theme of the next chapter.

Chapter 6

How should the agnostic live?

Practical atheism?

We can distinguish between two kinds of atheism: the theoretical and the practical. To be a theoretical atheist is to believe consciously that God does not exist. To be a practical atheist is to live without belief in God: to live a life in which the idea of God simply has no place. One can be a practical atheist without being a theoretical one (though to be a theoretical one without also being a practical one would be an odd combination).

How should the agnostic live? The obvious answer seems to be: as a practical atheist. (We're assuming here that the question concerns the kind of agnosticism that precludes belief; as we've already noted, one can believe that God exists without laying claim to *knowledge* that he does.) If the agnostic does not believe in God, then, so the argument goes, they will not do any of the things associated with that belief: engage in prayer, worship, read their experiences in a religious light, refer to religious ideas in deciding what they should do, and so on. And this, in effect, is a rejection, or an ignoring, of religion. Surely it would just be irrational to live a religious life, whilst not accepting the theoretical basis for such a life? Such a life, it seems, could only be based on self-deception. ('I do not believe, but I will pretend that

I do, and perhaps half-convince myself that I do.') And how could anyone rationally opt for a life of self-deception?

And yet those 19th-century agnostics, or some of them, were, apparently, religious. The poetry of the agnostics Arthur Hugh Clough (1819–61) and Matthew Arnold (1822–88) exhibits a religious response to the world. How is this possible? Could they not quite shake off the remains of the certainties of their youth? Or had they come to a different understanding of the nature of God? Can one be, theoretically speaking, an agnostic, but nevertheless be a *practical theist*? Let's compare and contrast the effects of agnosticism in two other areas: science and morality.

Science without belief?

How do you picture scientific progress? Is it like a growing museum collection, a gradual accretion of ideas and theories, only adopted after laborious testing, each theory somehow encompassing and improving on what has gone before? Or is a political simile more appropriate, in which science progresses by sudden and cataclysmic revolutions, sweeping aside old ideas by undermining their very assumptions and replacing them with radically new perspectives, based initially on little more than conjecture but perhaps subsequently vindicated by daring experiment? Perhaps we need both models, as each is descriptive of different episodes in the history of science. Take chemistry between 1830 and 1930, for instance. From the realization that the elements, if listed in terms of their atomic mass, exhibited certain repeated patterns, there emerged, in the work of Mendeleev, the formulation of the periodic law and its expression in the form of the Periodic Table, leading to the discovery of new elements, and the eventual explanation of periodicity in terms of the electronic model of the atom. Each step builds on its predecessor. But look at that same science in the previous 100 years, between 1730 and 1830, and you see two dramatic and revolutionary changes: one is the overthrowing of the old theory of combustion, based on the mythical substance phlogiston, by a new one, based on the newly discovered element oxygen; the second, the replacement of the vitalist conception of the difference between substances occurring in living creatures and those characteristic of the mineral world by the beginnings of organic chemistry. (No doubt, however, we could find examples of gradual changes in the earlier period and revolutionary ones in the second.)

The first model is conducive to a view of scientific progress as a gradual (and perhaps sometimes painful) approach to the truth. Perhaps we have not quite got there yet, but each new development takes us a little closer. At any rate, truth is the goal. The second model, while not inconsistent with that view, may make us rather more cautious about the pretensions of scientific theory to be even an approximation to the truth. Perhaps our currently cherished theories will be replaced by ones that, so far from being a refinement of those theories, require their total abandonment. Yet even abandoned theories have not necessarily been shown to be useless. They may function very well, even allowing us to make certain predications that turn out later to be vindicated. Newtonian physics may continue to be used to calculate motions and forces, even though it was as a theory superseded by relativistic physics. This suggests a picture of scientific progress as a search, not for the elusive truth, but rather for usefulness. The value of a theory lies in its power to enable us to predict phenomena and to manipulate the environment to our own ends. We can therefore use a theory, perhaps even being quite tenacious in our commitment to it, while remaining agnostic as to its truth.

Scientific agnosticism, therefore, is not incompatible with scientific activity and scientific progress. Indeed, such agnosticism may encourage an open-minded attitude, a willingness to accept phenomena which do not sit very well with the theory. Might we not draw a similar conclusion when it comes to religion? That might be a bit too hasty at this stage. Let's first consider another case, one quite removed from the scientific enterprise.

The moral outsider

The scientific agnostic who actively pursues the consequences of a scientific theory while remaining uncommitted to its truth may be an entirely intelligible figure. Indeed, this description may accurately portray the outlook of most working scientists. But what of the moral agnostic? This character does not know, on any moral issue whatsoever, what the correct answer is. He does not know, for instance, whether it would be right or wrong to tell a lie in such-a-such a situation, or whether it would be right or wrong to allow someone to die in some other situation. Now we, of course, would be moral agnostics in a wide range of situations: there are cases where we would just not know what the right thing to do would be. But we are not (if we are typical) morally agnostic in all situations, so we are imagining here a rather extreme case. How will this character, the total moral agnostic, live?

There can be no one answer to this question: it depends on his state of mind. He may be someone who is so anxious to do the right thing, and yet completely at a loss as to what the right thing is, that he ends up taking no decisive action at all, but is simply buffeted by circumstances, like the central character in Christopher Hampton's play *The Philanthropist*. In an inversion of Molière's *The Misanthrope*, Hampton's anagram-loving don Philip is anxious to please everybody and to offend nobody. Unfortunately, his failure to be guided by any stronger moral principle results in his offending everyone.

Or he may simply please himself, and be guided only by self-interest and (where necessary) convention, simply because he is not moved by the kinds of thoughts and feelings characteristic of moral behaviour. Albert Camus's *The Outsider* (*L'Étranger*) presents us, in Meursault, with the spectacle of someone who lacks the usual emotions towards others. His curious detachment is apparent from the opening words of the novel: 'Mother died today. Or, maybe, yesterday; I can't be sure.' On the day of his mother's funeral, he begins an affair with a girl he met at his office. He even agrees to marry her, but cannot make sense of her question 'Do you love me?' One day, finding himself threatened, he shoots someone in self-defence. But his apparent attacker was unarmed, and Meursault is tried for murder. Even with the prospect of a death sentence, he cannot feign emotions he does not feel, in order to win the jury's sympathy. His detachment is taken as evidence of guilt.

These two quite different portrayals of individuals we might with some justification describe as moral agnostics have something in common: it is hard to count much of their behaviour as *moral* behaviour. Nor is it necessarily immoral, though Meursault is apt to be interpreted as immoral. What characterizes his actions is their failure to be actuated by the relevant emotions. The engagement of appropriate feelings, rather than the emotionless following of a code of behaviour, is essential to truly moral agency. (We have to be careful how we express this, however. Perhaps the acquisition of moral feelings is itself a moral matter. And we certainly wouldn't suspend all moral judgement on someone simply because they were found to lack the relevant emotions.) The idea of a moral agnostic being a genuinely moral agent, then, seems questionable. The scientific agnostic can be a fully functioning scientist, since we can make sense of pursuing a theory for its usefulness. Emotions do not come into it, or if they do, they are not an essential part of the scientific attitude. But the total moral agnostic cannot be a fully functioning moral agent because, if they perform an act they do not believe is right or wrong, they are not activated by the moral impulse. This moral impulse, this feeling of being drawn towards an action because one's conscience impels one to do it, is not compatible with a complete detachment from the question of whether it is right or wrong.

Pascal's Wager and James's defence

With the contrast between the scientific and the moral agnostic in mind, let us look at a famous, indeed notorious, argument for faith known as Pascal's Wager. Pascal begins by reminding us of our limitations in deciding the question of God's existence:

> If there is a God, he is infinitely beyond our comprehension, since, being indivisible and without limits, he bears no relation to us. We are therefore incapable of knowing either what he is or whether he is ... 'Either God is or he is not'. But to which view shall we be inclined? Reason cannot decide this question. Infinite chaos separates us. At the far end of this infinite distance a coin is being spun which will come down heads or tails. How will you wager?

Perhaps the rational thing to do is not to wager at all. But not to wager is effectively to wager that God does not exist. In contrast:

> Let us weigh up the gain and loss involved in calling heads that God exists. Let us assess the two cases: if you win you win everything, if you lose you lose nothing. Do not hesitate then; wager that he does exist.

If you win, you win everything. That is, you win eternal life in heaven. This is not, note, a reason for thinking it *true* that God exists, but rather a reason for thinking it better to believe than not to believe. Or rather (since belief cannot be summoned up at will), it is better to act in such a way – living the religious life – that belief will eventually come.

Recall William James's appeal to our passional nature in approaching religious belief (see Chapter 5). Aren't James and Pascal proposing something similar? James, however, doesn't entirely approve of Pascal's proposal, with its apparent shameless appeal to self-interest. Pascal's talk of 'winning' or 'losing' a wager does, admittedly, smack of a base form of self-interest. But that depends on whether you view heaven as a garden of earthly and sensuous delights or as perfect communion with God. Is it mere self-interest to want the best, most exalted kind of existence of which humans are capable? However, James's main objection to the Wager is that it seems a wholly cold-blooded calculation, an acceptance of faith for the benefits it brings, rather than a passionate commitment to something for its own sake. Adopting the religious life on the basis of such a calculation is comparable to the scientific agnostic's adoption of a scientific theory in order to exploit its usefulness. But whereas the scientific agnostic really can be a scientist, the religious agnostic (according to James's picture of the matter) cannot lead a truly religious life. Science can be done without emotion; religion cannot. The religious agnostic seems to be in the same position as the moral agnostic: just as the latter cannot engage in genuinely moral action, so the former cannot engage in a genuinely religious life. Despite the impression given by the wager, Pascal himself took a far from detached view of faith: for him, it was indeed a matter of passionate commitment and total belief.

Pascal's Wager could be seen as an attempt to induce the agnostic to take the leap of faith. James, in contrast, is not addressing the agnostic in such terms. His point is not that the agnostic should take the plunge, and accept faith for the benefits it brings, but rather that if James, moved by his passional rather than his rational nature, believes in God, then he cannot be criticized by the agnostic. The agnostic, says James, will not believe, because of an attachment to the principle that one should only believe what one has sufficient evidence to believe. But that principle itself is not justified by reason, and attachment to it is just another case of being moved by one's feelings – in this case, by a fear of believing a falsehood. James offers, not an inducement to the agnostic, but rather a defence of faith against the agnostic's doubts.

Love of the unknown

James is surely right that belief in God, as a truly religious response to the world, must engage our emotions – that it is, in part, an emotional response to the world. It is not like a scientific hypothesis, and treating it as if it were casts it in a rather poor light. As atheists are quick to point out, as an explanation, the God hypothesis is not particularly informative. Belief in God is more of a belief *that there is* an explanation of a particular sort, one that takes love and intelligence to be among the most fundamental components of reality, even if we don't fully understand that explanation, or see clearly how it is to be reconciled with what looks on the face of it like falsifying evidence. What makes this trust that there is such an explanation so much more significant than a trust that there is an explanation of matter which underlies both cosmology and quantum physics, is the focus for our emotions that the idea of God provides.

But that focus leaves quite a lot that is unknown. Love of God is largely love of the unknown God. So even within religious faith there can be, indeed must be, a significant amount of agnosticism, agnosticism about the details of God's nature. It might seem puzzling that, if the idea of God is so nebulous, it should nevertheless be a focus of intense feeling. But that is because the notion of God is already tied up with, is defined through, highly emotive matters: one's love for others, the desire for ultimate purpose in life, the voice of conscience.

All that, of course, is from within the theistic point of view. It might be argued that the true agnostic is outside all that, and so unable to engage at the appropriate emotional level. Of course, there is nothing to stop the agnostic observing the rituals of the religious life: attending church services, reading religious texts, even praying. But won't there always be a detachment, a sense of being outside looking in, and won't the apparent following of a religious life necessarily be merely experimental and provisional? 'I'll go along with this until either something happens or I realize that it won't, and I can give the experiment up as a failure.' Of course, if something does happen, as Pascal suggests it will, and I find myself really believing, then I will be living an authentic religious life – but then, it seems I will have abandoned my agnosticism.

There is, however, a very familiar phenomenon in which strong emotions are accompanied by suspension of belief: our responses to fiction. It is reported that when the instalment of *Oliver Twist* in which Nancy is brutally beaten to death by Bill Sykes was first published, in *Bentley's Miscellany*, a number of readers fainted with the shock. We may be rather more hardened and desensitized readers nowadays, but fiction has retained its power to shock, terrify, sadden, and move. Moreover, fiction can evoke moral sentiments: we may approve, or disapprove, of a fictional character's actions. Or we may sympathize with a character's moral dilemma. How is it that fiction can provoke this kind of response? After all, we know, while we are reading or watching it, that it does not portray real events. One possibility is that it directs our attention to abstract truths about human nature which, when we contemplate them, become objects of our emotions. *Lord of the Flies* may disturb us because it reveals a discomforting possibility about the nature of childhood. But that cannot be the whole story, as our emotions are often attached to a particular character: I feel sorry for Piggy, not just sorry that children can sometimes be cruel to those who are perceived as different. Perhaps, then, our emotions are engaged by fiction because we temporarily forget that it is fictional: we suspend our disbelief. But that seems questionable, too, since at no point would we be disposed to say that what we are engaging with is real. A frightening film portraying a lurking menace in every electrical appliance will not make us behave towards those appliances as we would if we really believed in such a menace (though we may feel a little less comfortable when we next put the kettle on).

There is, then, something of a puzzle as to why fictions are capable of provoking the emotions that they do. But the phenomenon itself is incontestable. Now translate this to the religious sphere. Perhaps we are watching one of the York Mystery Plays, portraying the arrest, trial, and crucifixion of Jesus. It would be odd if such a performance did not evoke strong emotions. But now suppose, instead of being passive spectators, we were to engage in a religious ritual, or narrative, *as a game of make-believe*. Perhaps 'game' has the wrong kind of connotations here, as the language and images that typify religious ritual are not particularly game-like. But the point is that we engage in it as we would were we to take part in a play. Now, if we are sufficiently caught up, not only in the drama that is unfolding around us, but in our own roles in that drama, would our emotions not be aroused as deeply, if not more, as when we were merely onlookers? Perhaps, in order for us to immerse ourselves entirely, we have to forget that it is fiction that we are engaging in. But whatever the mental mechanism, there is every reason to suppose that participating in religion as fiction would be capable of evoking the same kind of emotional response as does our participating in other kinds of fiction.

Now let's take a further step, and suppose that, while engaged in the fiction, we realize that we *don't know* whether it is fictional or not. Or rather, although we are pretty sure that some elements will be fictional, there are other, perhaps more central, elements that may not be. What effect will that have on our emotional engagement? It can't, surely, diminish it. The hold that fiction has on us could only be increased if there were a sense that elements of it might correspond to reality. But this is precisely the agnostic's position. There are parts of any religion which are fictional embellishments. But, at least in the case of the great religions, it cannot be demonstrated that the whole is a fiction. Would acceptance of a religion on such terms count as a genuine religious response? There seems no reason why not. After all, the theist will typically be agnostic about certain aspects of their religion: perhaps this particular component is true, perhaps not. And yet the whole religious fabric, with its distinctive language, history, morality, and images, is embraced as a seamless whole, not neatly partitioned into the parts the theist is prepared to say he knows are true (and which evoke the strongest responses) and those about which he admits uncertainty (and towards which he consequently feels a certain detachment). The emotional commitment is towards the whole. So, even for the theist, such commitment is compatible with a degree of agnosticism. The religious agnostic is simply extending the area over which that attitude is taken.

A religious life, then, is possible for the agnostic, and not simply as a cautious, experimental, and ultimately detached affair. But of course it is not obligatory. Many agnostics may find that they are psychologically unable to take this imaginative and emotional step.

Chapter 7
How should agnosticism be taught?

The battle of the buses

In late 2008, a number of buses appeared in London carrying the slogan 'There's probably no God. Now stop worrying and enjoy your life.' By the beginning of 2009, similar 'atheist buses' were appearing in other UK cities. This was the result of a successful campaign, supported by the British Humanist Association, which raised more than £140,000 to fund the adverts. Eventually, no fewer than 800 of these buses were doing the rounds, and their counterparts were appearing in Spain and Russia. It was, the organizers explained, an antidote to what they saw as Christian propaganda in various forms, sometimes (it was alleged) with the unsettling suggestion that eternal damnation lay in store for unbelievers. The atheist adverts were intended to assure atheists and agnostics that it was entirely acceptable not to believe in God. Predictably, there was a religious response, and by February, 175 London buses were carrying the slogan 'There definitely is a God. So join the Christian Party and enjoy your life.' The Advertising Standards Authority, meanwhile, had received numerous complaints from Christians objecting to the atheist adverts, but the ASA ruled that the advertisements were 'an expression of the advertiser's opinion and…the claims in it were not capable of objective substantiation'. It is intriguing to find atheist (and, by extension, theist) advertisements being condoned on agnostic grounds.

Were the complainants justified? Is this an acceptable way of spreading these kinds of messages? Slogans on buses seem no different in principle to speeches from soap boxes, party political broadcasts, or posters outside Evangelical churches. They preach to the converted, and the unconverted will view them with appropriate caution. Advertisements are expressions of opinion, value-laden, and often – as the ASA recognizes – not easily verified. Some even invite one *not* to take them at face value, such as the Strand cigarette television advertisements of the 1950s, in which a palpably lonely man in a raincoat lights up a cigarette in a deserted street, while the voice-over declares 'You're never alone with a Strand.' Suppose we took this announcement at face value. Consider the possible implications: that with a Strand cigarette, you're always with another human being (false), or that you're always accompanied by a cigarette (trivial), or that you are always in the presence of some invisible and intangible being (strange and unsettling). Evidently, the power of the advertisement lies in its *not* being taken at face value. (Unfortunately, however, its audience tended to associate Strand cigarettes with lonely men, and the brand was withdrawn within a few years.) It is unlikely, then, whichever side one happens to be on, that anyone was in danger of being seriously misled by either the pro-atheist or pro-theist bus advertisements.

What *would* be undesirable would be the bombardment of the public by absolutely uniform messages, such as those dinned out on telescreens in George Orwell's *Nineteen Eighty-Four*. It is the fact that we encounter conflicting images and messages that forces us to think for ourselves, to realize that there are some matters on which we cannot simply rely on someone else's judgement. This is one answer to the commentator who worried about the effect the atheist bus slogans might have on children (who nevertheless appear sufficiently robust to withstand the bewildering variety of messages from the media with which they spend so much time).

Should there be an agnostic slogan on buses, too? 'We can't work out whether there's a God or not' somehow lacks the punch of its

11. Taking the message to London's streets: Richard Dawkins and the 'atheist bus' campaign

rivals. The real value of agnosticism is not so much the agnostic conclusion as the route taken to get there, and this depends on accepting the agnostic principle: do not pretend to knowledge when the basis for your belief is shown to be inadequate. This is an important educational principle. So, how should agnosticism be presented in education?

Uncertainty and creativity

Perhaps a better agnostic slogan would be 'Uncertainty is good for you!' For agnosticism is just one instance of the wider phenomenon of uncertainty. Uncertainty tends to be seen as a bad thing, something we should seek to eliminate or reduce. Not having that vital piece of information can be a source of anxiety. Not knowing what to believe, we are confined to inaction. Or are we? Uncertainty, it can be shown, is one source of creativity. Sometimes we can improve our situation *without* eliminating the uncertainty.

Unseen by you, a coin is placed under one of three cups. You have to guess which cup hides the coin, and if you guess correctly, the coin is yours. So you go ahead and choose. Without further information, the chances that you have picked the right cup is one in three. Now one of the cups not hiding the coin is removed, leaving you with just two cups, including the cup you chose. You are then invited to make a further decision: stick with your original choice, or switch to the other cup. It might seem that it doesn't matter what you decide, since staying or switching both risk getting it wrong. In fact, however, whereas sticking with your original choice doesn't change your original chance of success (since a cup was removed only after you chose), switching now gives you an improved chance of being right, since there are now only two cups. This may sound like a piece of statistical sophistry, but the results over a large enough series of choices vindicate it. We can, after all, respond positively to uncertainty without getting rid of it.

Here is another, rather more bizarre, example. In 'A Question of Identity', the neurologist Oliver Sacks describes a conversation with a patient suffering from Korsakov's syndrome, robbing him of the power to form long-term memories. The patient, dubbed William Thompson by Sacks, can remember his former employment as a grocer, but can remember nothing about what led to his being admitted to an institution. Greeting Sacks, he first takes him to be a customer, and then as an old friend, Tom Pitkin. When Sacks tells him he is not Tom Pitkin, Thompson (seeing the white coat) suggests he's the local butcher, and then a doctor, then a psychiatrist…

> He remembered nothing for more than a few seconds. He was continually disoriented. Abysses of amnesia continually opened beneath him, but he would bridge them, nimbly, by fluent confabulations and fictions of all kinds. For him they were not fictions, but how he suddenly saw, or interpreted, the world … it was not a tissue of ever-changing, evanescent fancies and illusion, but a wholly normal, stable and factual world. So far as *he* was concerned, there was nothing the matter.

In the face of massive loss of information, which would otherwise threaten to make life intolerable, Thompson's endlessly creative confabulation is effectively a survival strategy, an attempt to impose normality. And although this is clearly a pathological case, it tells us something about our own in-built ability to cope with uncertainty, the capacity to generate a whole series of competing hypotheses about the world – hypotheses which in ordinary circumstances are selected or rejected on the basis of subsequent information. The more we are able to cope with uncertainty, the more effective we are likely to be. It is for good reason that some psychometric tests include questions designed to measure a subject's intolerance of uncertainty.

Uncertainty can also lead to theoretical progress, not simply because of the need to reduce uncertainty by developing better theories and acquiring more information, but because uncertainty itself can be made the subject of theory, helping us to decide what to do in the face of that uncertainty. Take the famous puzzle of the prisoner's dilemma. Two prisoners have been convicted of committing some crime together. Each is told that if he confesses, and the other remains silent, the confessor will be released immediately and the other imprisoned for ten years. If both remain silent, they will both be imprisoned for six months. If both confess, they will both be imprisoned for five years. What should each do? They cannot meet to confer, so each must come to a decision without knowing what the other has decided. In deciding what to do, each prisoner has to think not only of what would be the best outcome for him, but also how the other prisoner is likely to reach a decision. The problem may be an artificial one, but it mirrors real-life situations where there are competing interests, and no-one has complete information about what each interested party intends to do. A sobering example of such a real-life situation was the nuclear arms race of the 1950s. By the beginning of that decade, the United States and the Soviet Union both knew that each had the capacity to launch a devastating nuclear attack on the other, but neither knew the other side's intentions. It was suggested by some prominent commentators that America should launch an unprovoked, pre-emptive strike, to avoid becoming the victim. Fortunately, that argument did not prevail. A more recent example, still generating debate, was the Anglo-American invasion of Iraq in 2003, although in this case uncertainty about intentions was (as became evident) compounded on one side by imperfect information about the other's capacity to engage in nuclear and biological warfare.

The need to put decision-making under conditions of uncertainty on a rational basis led to the development of *game theory*, initiated by the French mathematician Émile Borel in a 1921 paper of that name, but given sophisticated mathematical treatment by John von Neumann (one of the proponents of a preventative strike by the US on the USSR) between 1928 and his early death in 1957. Neumann saw the application to a variety of fields, including military strategy and economics, and in 1941 published, with Oskar Morgenstern, the influential *Theory of Games and Economic Behaviour*.

Economics is one example of our creative response to uncertainty, seeking not merely to eliminate it, but to learn to live with it, turning it to our advantage. Religion is another example. Not knowing how the world came into being, what the ultimate purpose of life is, and the source of our sense of goodness, different ages and cultures have produced astonishingly rich stories which combine these mysteries into a unified whole, and give life a shape and meaning. That is not to say that they are *nothing more than* stories, but rather that we don't know which aspects of them penetrate to the core of reality. That is the agnostic conclusion. It is not a critique of religion, but a recognition of its true nature: a creative and life-enhancing response to uncertainty.

Uncertainty and tolerance: agnostic education

In the light of what has just been said, I am suggesting that agnosticism should be presented as something positive, not simply a shrugging of the shoulders, but an honest recognition of uncertainty, where uncertainty itself is shown to have benefits: coping with uncertainty makes us more creative, more resilient, and leads to genuine intellectual progress. It also makes us more *tolerant*, and this is the key to understanding what effect agnosticism should have on religious education.

Let's approach the issue by asking what is wrong with the bleakly fact-oriented schooling parodied in Dickens' *Hard Times*:

> 'Now, what I want is, Facts. Teach these boys and girls nothing but Facts. Facts alone are wanted in life. Plant nothing else, and root out everything else. You can only form the minds of reasoning animals upon Facts: nothing else will ever be of any service to them. This is the principle on which I bring up my own children, and this is the principle on which I bring up these children. Stick to Facts, sir!'

Thus Thomas Gradgrind advises the schoolmaster M'Choakumchild, who, having been brought up on the same principle, readily obliges. It is not just the lack of any human interest in being made to recite the definition of horse as 'graminivorous quadruped with hard hooves, etc.' which illustrates the sterility of this approach, but the idea that education is a matter simply of learning things known to be true. History (to alight on a particular example) can be and often was taught in this way in schools, but the more enlightened technique that happily now prevails teaches an awareness of how our view of the past is informed by an interpretation of necessarily limited and sometimes, in the case of written records, biased sources. That is how students come to recognize the fallibility of beliefs about the past, and learn to be receptive to other interpretations.

Applied to religious education, the contrast would be between the teaching of a single set of religious dogmas in a way that does not invite questioning of them, and showing how religious beliefs in different cultures have arisen from various sources, and the grounds on which their authority is supposed to rest. To adopt that second approach is not just to teach agnosticism alongside systems of religious belief, it is in effect to take an agnostic approach towards the teaching of those systems.

Two apparent implications of this should be resisted. The first is that agnosticism must be hostile to 'faith schools', that is, those schools whose children are explicitly educated within the framework of a particular religion. The agnostic is not necessarily hostile to religion. Quite the reverse: as I have argued, we can make perfect sense of embracing religious discourse and practice even from an agnostic perspective. The essence of religion does not consist of reciting religious dogmas as if they were unshakeable truths, known without a shred of doubt to be true, and it would be undesirable for faith schools to take this line. It would also be undesirable if they ignored, or were critical of, other religious or humanistic perspectives. A truly religious education teaches religious tolerance.

The second apparent implication which must be resisted is that, if they truly desire an open-minded education for their children, agnostics should join those religious groups who ask for creationism to be taught in biology classes as a rival to evolution theory. Agnostics about the existence of God do not have to be equally agnostic about every controversy that involves God. It depends on how specific the controversy is. They may think, for example, that the 'Young Earth' creationist's assertion that all the species of life that currently populate the planet were created just as they are, in all their complexity, about 6,000 years ago, is, given the evidence, far less probable than the evolutionist's assertion that complex life forms evolved gradually from much simpler forms as a result of genetic mutation and natural selection. They may also think that appealing to a religious text as the basis for asserting creationism is clearly non-scientific. In contrast, they may believe that the much more general hypothesis that the universe was the result of intelligent design is as likely to be true as its denial, but also think that so general a hypothesis has no place in science classes. You don't have to describe the intelligent design hypothesis as 'not science' to exclude it from the biology classroom. Intelligent design has often been put forward in response to evidence which emerges from scientific inquiry (such as the 'fine-tuning' considerations discussed in Chapter 4). But so general a hypothesis, from which (as the agnostic will note) it is very hard to generate specific testable predictions, will not be a paradigm of the kinds of explanations dealt with in biology. What the agnostic should desire is that these issues be discussed somewhere in the curriculum.

An agnostic manifesto

Let's end by summarizing the agnostic outlook. My portrait of it will not perhaps be accepted in all details by all agnostics, but

I propose the following as an 'agnostic manifesto', embodying the conclusions reached at various points in this brief study:

(1) As far as the onus of proof is concerned, the theist and atheist are in exactly the same position: neither has a greater duty to justify their position than the other. There should be no automatic presumption of atheism, but rather an initial presumption of agnosticism.

(2) Theism is not 'bad science'; it is the very general hypothesis that there exists, in terms of an intelligent being, a true unifying explanation of the world, ourselves, our consciousness, and our capacity for good. The initial probability of the proposition that there exists such an explanation (as opposed to a detailed attempt at one) is not smaller than the initial probability of the proposition that there exists no such explanation.

(3) The agnostic principle: always seek reasons for beliefs, and do not make knowledge claims that are not adequately supported by the evidence. Clifford's statement of this principle, that 'it is wrong, always, everywhere, and for anyone, to believe anything upon insufficient evidence', is too strong. Clifford does not allow for *degrees* of belief: we should proportion the extent to which we are inclined to believe something to the weight of the evidence.

(4) The evidence which is often pointed to as supporting, or undermining, theism, is ambiguous: it can be shown to be consistent both with theism and atheism without resorting to *ad hoc* or implausible manoeuvres.

(5) Since the evidence is ambiguous, commitment either to theism or atheism is, at least in part, an emotional response to the world, not a purely rational one. But this does not make either theism or atheism an *irrational* response. Theists regard the religious attitude as natural, in-built, and one which is valuable and to be encouraged and developed. Atheists, while often recognizing the response as natural, see it as apt to delude us, and as something to be exorcised. The difference is more temperamental than either side typically acknowledges.

(6) Agnosticism as an attitude should not be viewed as final, but provisional, to be accompanied by an open-minded attitude, and a willingness to look at new evidence and arguments.

(7) There are different shades of agnosticism, reflecting different views on how probable or improbable theism is. The admission that one doesn't know whether or not God exists is entirely compatible with either a theist or an atheist outlook. There can be belief without knowledge.

(8) Even the kind of agnosticism that takes theism and atheism to be equiprobable is compatible with a practical and emotional commitment to a religious way of life. James thought that such commitment necessitated genuine belief, but the agnostic participation in religion is more akin to participation in a game of make-believe.

(9) Agnosticism is part of the wider phenomenon of uncertainty, and uncertainty is positive in so far as it promotes creativity, theoretical progress, and social tolerance. Agnosticism thus promotes religious pluralism: peaceful co-existence between different religious faiths, and between religious and humanist groups. What it does *not* promote or imply is a relativistic view of truth: 'Islam is true-for-me but false-for-you', and so on.

Given the benefits noted in (9), an education based on the above tenets would be a genuinely humanizing one.

We began this study with Adam's first recorded act in the Garden of Eden: the naming of living creatures. We end with his last: accepting from the serpent-bewitched Eve the fruit of the Tree of Knowledge. 'And the eyes of them both were opened, and they knew that they were naked.' For this, they are banished from the Garden. Eating the forbidden fruit may have brought them knowledge of good and evil, but, judging by the history of mankind, it also brought them uncertainty and doubt. Might that uncertainty and doubt not be, after all, the divine gift to mankind?

References

Given here are bibliographical details just of those passages quoted in the text. More extensive references are provided in the 'Further Reading' section.

Introduction

'And out of the ground...': Genesis 2.19
'The robust Muscular Christian...': Richard Dawkins, *The God Delusion* (London: Black Swan, 2006), p. 69
'there is nothing wrong...': Dawkins, *The God Delusion*, p. 70
'contrast the great certainties...': J. K. Galbraith, *Age of Uncertainty* (London: Book Club Associates, 1977), p. 7

Chapter 1

'Therefore, Lord, not only...': Anselm, *Proslogion*, ed. and tr. M. J. Charlesworth (Oxford: Clarendon Press, 1965), Chapter XV
'A mere man cannot see...': St Thomas Aquinas, *Summa Theologiae*, Vol. 3., ed. and tr. Herbert McCabe (London: Eyre and Spottiswoode, 1964), Part 1, question 12, article 11
'the very idea of evidence...': Dawkins, *The God Delusion*, p. 70

Chapter 2

'Then Paul stood...': Acts of the Apostles 17.22–3
'a great and even severe Agnostic...': R. H. Hutton, 'Pope Huxley', *Spectator*, 43, January 1870, pp. 135–6

'Agnosticism is not properly described...': T. H. Huxley, 'Agnosticism and Christianity', in *Collected Essays*, Vol. V: *Science and Christian Tradition* (London: Macmillan, 1904), p. 310

'I do not very much care...': T. H. Huxley, 'Agnosticism and Christianity', p. 311

'interrupted my dogmatic slumber': Immanuel Kant, *Prolegomena to Any Future Metaphysics That Will Be Able to Present Itself as a Science*, tr. Peter G. Lucas (Manchester: Manchester University Press, 1953), p. 9

'great propensity to spread itself...': David Hume, *Treatise of Human Nature*, ed. L. A. Selby-Bigge and P. H. Nidditch (Oxford: Oxford University Press, 1978), Book I, Part III, §14, p. 167

'the parent of Kant...': T. H. Huxley, *Hume* (London: Macmillan, 1895), p. 70

'In a word, Cleanthes...': David Hume, *Dialogues Concerning Natural Religion*, ed. Martin Bell (London: Penguin, 1990), Part V

'an ability to set out oppositions...': Sextus Empiricus, *Outlines of Scepticism*, ed. Julia Annas and Jonathan Barnes (Cambridge: Cambridge University Press, 2000), Book I, p. iv

Chapter 3

'"Show me", you say...': Carl Sagan, *The Demon-Haunted World: Science as a Candle in the Dark* (London: Headline, 1997), p. 171

'the only sensible approach...': Carl Sagan, *The Demon-Haunted World*, p. 171

'Many orthodox people...': Bertrand Russell, 'Is There a God?', in *The Collected Essays of Bertrand Russell*, ed. John G. Slater (London and New York: Routledge, 1997), pp. 547–8

'Many different definitions...': Anthony Kenny, *What I Believe* (London: Continuum, 2006), p. 21

Chapter 4

'Hear me, O LORD...': I Kings 18

'These feelings in us...': John Henry Newman, *An Essay in Aid of a Grammar of Assent*, ed. Ian Ker (Oxford: Clarendon Press, 1985), p. 110

'At first I began to feel...': quoted in William James, *The Varieties of Religious Experience* (New York: Longmans, Green and Co., 1902), p. 191

'To consider the world...': John Henry Newman, *Apologia Pro Vita Sua*, ed. Ian Ker (London: Penguin, 1994), p. 217

'Man he made to serve him wittily...': Robert Bolt, *A Man For All Seasons*, Act Two

Chapter 5

'...if "god" is a metaphysical term...': A. J. Ayer, *Language, Truth and Logic* (London: Victor Gollancz, 1936), p. 115

'...I was, at that time, in Germany...': René Descartes, *Discourse on Method* (London: Penguin, 1968), p. 35

'It is wrong, always, everywhere...': William Clifford, 'The Ethics of Belief', reprinted in *Stuart Brown, Philosophy of Religion: An Introduction with Readings* (London: Routledge, 2001), p. 168

'Here, in this room...': William James, 'The Will to Believe', in *The Will to Believe and Other Essays in Popular Philosophy* (New York: Longmans, Green and Co., 1905), p. 9

Chapter 6

'Mother died today...': Albert Camus, *The Outsider* (London: Penguin, 1961), p. 1

'If there is a God...': Blaise Pascal, *Pensées* (London: Penguin, 1966), p. 122

'Let us weigh up the gain...': Blaise Pascal, *Pensées*, p. 123

Chapter 7

'an expression of the advertiser's opinion...': Advertising Standards Agency, ASA news archive, 21 January 2009

'He remembered nothing...': Oliver Sacks, *The Man Who Mistook His Wife for a Hat* (London: Pan Books, 1985), p. 104

'Now, what I want is, Facts...': Charles Dickens, *Hard Times*, chapter 1

'And the eyes of them both were opened...': Genesis 3.7

Further reading

General

Early discussions of agnosticism

Penelope Fitzgerald, *A Protest Against Agnosticism: The Rationale or Philosophy of Belief* (London: Kegan Paul, 1890)

Thomas Henry Huxley, *Collected Essays*, Vol. 5: *Science and Christian Tradition* (London: Macmillan, 1904)

Jacob Gould Schurman, *Agnosticism and Religion* (New York: Charles Scribner's Sons, 1896)

Leslie Stephen, *An Agnostic's Apology, and Other Essays* (London: Smith Elder, 1893)

Henry Wace, *Christianity and Agnosticism: Reviews of Some Recent Attacks on the Christian Faith* (Edinburgh and London: William Blackwood & Sons, 1895)

James Ward, *Naturalism and Agnosticism: The Gifford Lectures Delivered before the University of Aberdeen in the Years 1896–1898* (London: A & C Black, 1903)

Contemporary discussions of agnosticism

Piers Benn, 'Some Uncertainties About Agnosticism', *International Journal for the Philosophy of Religion*, 46 (1999), 171–88

H. J. Blackham, 'What is Agnosticism?', *Free Inquiry*, 1 (1981), 31–3

Alan Brinton, 'The Reasonableness of Agnosticism', *Religious Studies*, 20 (1984), 627–30

Alan Brinton, 'Agnosticism and Atheism', *Sophia*, 28 (1989), 2–6

Clement Dore, 'Agnosticism', *Religious Studies*, 18 (1982), 503–7

Henry Jacoby, 'Is Agnosticism Unreasonable?', *Sophia*, 30 (1991), 35–41

Anthony Kenny, *Faith and Reason* (New York: Columbia University Press, 1983)

Anthony Kenny, *The Unknown God: Agnostic Essays* (London and New York: Continuum, 2004)

Anthony Kenny, *What I Believe* (London and New York: Continuum, 2006)

Kenneth Kondyk, 'Evidentialist Agnosticism', *Religious Studies* (1991), 319–32

Robert McLauglin, 'Necessary Agnosticism?', *Analysis*, 44 (1984), 198–202

P. J. McGrath, 'Atheism or Agnosticism?', *Analysis*, 47 (1987), 54–7

Thomas Morris, 'Agnosticism', *Analysis*, 45 (1985), 219–24

Graham Oppy, 'Weak Agnosticism Defended', *International Journal for the Philosophy of Religion*, 36 (1994), 147–67

Andrew Pyle (ed.), *Agnosticism: Contemporary Responses to Spencer and Huxley* (Bristol: Thoemmes, 1995)

Thomas McHugh Reed, 'Christianity and Agnosticism', *International Journal for the Philosophy of Religion*, 52 (2002), 81–95

Sven Rosenkranz, 'Agnosticism as a Third Stance', *Mind*, 116 (2007), 55–104

Patrick A. Woods, 'From the Middle Out: A Case for Agnosticism', *Sophia*, 46 (2007), 35–48

William Henry Young, 'Evangelical Agnosticism', *Free Inquiry*, 5 (1983)

Encyclopaedia articles

Thomas Dixon, 'Agnosticism', *New Dictionary of the History of Ideas*, ed. Maryanne Cline Horowitz (New York: Charles Scribner's Sons, 2005)

A. G. N. Flew, 'Agnosticism', under 'Religious and Spiritual Belief, Systems of', *Encyclopaedia Britannica* (Chicago: Encyclopaedia Britannica Inc., 15th edn., 2005)

Alfred E. Garvie, 'Agnosticism', *Encyclopedia of Religion and Ethics*, ed. James Hastings (New York: Charles Scribner's Sons, 1928)

Ronald Hepburn, 'Agnosticism', *The Encyclopedia of Philosophy*, ed. Paul Edwards (New York: Macmillan, 1968)

William L. Rowe, 'Agnosticism', *Routledge Encyclopedia of Philosophy*, ed. Edward Craig (London: Routledge, 1998)

Edmund Shanahan, 'Agnosticism', *Catholic Encyclopedia*, ed. Charles G. Herbermann (London: Caxton Publishing, 1907) <http://www.newadvent.org/cathen/01215c.htm>

J. J. C. Smart, 'Atheism and Agnosticism', *Stanford Encyclopedia of Philosophy*, ed. Edward N. Zalta (online resource) <http://plato.stanford.edu/entries/atheism-agnosticism/>

Chapter 1

Atheism and theism

Julian Baggini, *Atheism: A Very Short Introduction* (Oxford: Oxford University Press, 2003)

Richard Dawkins, *The God Delusion* (London: Black Swan, 2006)

Richard M. Gale, *On the Nature and Existence of God* (Cambridge: Cambridge University Press, 1991)

Michael Martin, *Atheism: A Philosophical Justification* (Philadelphia: Temple University Press, 1990)

Alister McGrath, *Dawkins' God: Genes, Memes and the Meaning of Life* (Oxford: Blackwell, 2004)

J. J. C. Smart and John Haldane, *Atheism and Theism*, 2nd edn. (Oxford: Blackwell, 2003)

Richard Swinburne, *Is There a God?* (Oxford: Oxford University Press, 1996)

Chapter 2

Victorian agnostics

Noel Annan, *Leslie Stephen: The Godless Victorian* (London: Weidenfield and Nicolson, 1984)

Don Cupitt, 'Mansel's Theory of Regulative Truth', *Journal of Theological Studies*, 18 (1967), 104–26

Adrian Desmond, *Huxley: From Devil's Disciple to Evolution's High Priest* (London: Penguin, 1998)

Timothy Fitzgerald, 'Herbert Spencer's Agnosticism', *Religious Studies*, 23 (1987), 477–91

Timothy Fitzgerald, 'Mansel's Agnosticism', *Religious Studies* (1990), 525–41

Bernard Lightman, *The Origins of Agnosticism: Victorian Unbelief and the Limits of Knowledge* (Baltimore and London: The Johns Hopkins University Press, 1987)

Bernard Lightman, 'Huxley and Scientific Agnosticism: The Strange History of a Failed Rhetorical Strategy', *British Journal for the History of Science*, 35 (2002), 271–89

Paul White, *Thomas Huxley: Making the 'Man of Science'* (Cambridge: Cambridge University Press, 2003)

James Woelfel, 'Victorian Agnosticism and Liberal Theology', *American Journal of Theology and Philosophy*, 19 (1997), 61–76

Philosophical precursors

A. J. Ayer, *Hume* (Oxford: Oxford University Press, 1980)

Peter Byrne, *Kant on God* (Aldershot: Ashgate, 2007)

J. C. A. Gaskin, *Hume's Philosophy of Religion*, 2nd edn. (Basingstoke: Macmillan, 1988)

Roger Scruton, *Kant* (Oxford: Oxford University Press, 1982)

Sextus Empiricus, *Outlines of Scepticism*, ed. Julia Annas and Jonathan Barnes (Cambridge: Cambridge University Press, 2000)

Chapter 3

Russell on religion

Bertrand Russell, *Why I Am Not a Christian, and Other Essays on Religion and Related Subjects* (London: Unwin, 1957)

The presumption of atheism

Anthony Flew, 'The Presumption of Atheism', *Canadian Journal of Philosophy*, 2 (1972), 29–49

Scott Shalkowski, 'Atheological Apologetics', *American Philosophical Quarterly*, 26 (1989), 1–17

Chapter 4

Arguments from design and fine-tuning

Paul Davies, *The Accidental Universe* (Cambridge: Cambridge University Press, 1982)

John Leslie, *Universes* (London: Routledge, 1989)

Richard Swinburne, *The Existence of God* (Oxford: Clarendon Press, 1978)

Biological accounts of intelligence and morality

Richard Dawkins, *The Selfish Gene* (Oxford: Oxford University Press, 1976)

Richard Dawkins, *The Blind Watchmaker* (Harlow: Longman, 1986)

Daniel Dennett, *Darwin's Dangerous Idea* (New York: Simon and Schuster, 1995)

Moral theories

Simon Blackburn, *Ethics: A Very Short Introduction* (Oxford: Oxford University Press, 2001)

J. L. Mackie, *Ethics: Inventing Right and Wrong* (Harmondsworth: Penguin, 1977)

Charles L. Stevenson, *Ethics and Language* (New Haven: Yale University Press, 1944)

Religious experience

William James, *The Varieties of Religious Experience* (London: Longmans Green, 1902; reissued as a Penguin paperback 1985)

Keith E. Yandell, *The Epistemology of Religious Experience* (Cambridge: Cambridge University Press, 1993)

The problem of evil

Marilyn McCord Adams and Robert Merrihew Adams (eds.), *The Problem of Evil* (Oxford: Oxford University Press, 1990)

Peter van Inwagen, *The Problem of Evil* (Oxford: Clarendon Press, 2006)

Chapter 5

Logical positivism

A. J. Ayer, *Language, Truth and Logic* (London: Victor Gollancz, 1936)

Karl Popper, *Conjectures and Refutations: The Growth of Scientific Knowledge* (London: Routledge and Kegan Paul, 1963)

Religious non-realism

Richard Braithwaite, 'An Empiricist's View of the Nature of Religious Belief', in *The Philosophy of Religion*, ed. Basil Mitchell (Oxford: Oxford University Press, 1970), pp. 72–91

Don Cupitt, *The Sea of Faith* (London: BBC, 1984)

Antony Flew, R. M. Hare, and Basil Mitchell, 'Theology and Falsification', in *The Philosophy of Religion*, ed. Basil Mitchell (Oxford: Oxford University Press, 1970), pp. 13–22

John A. T. Robinson, *Honest to God* (London: SCM, 1963)

Ludwig Wittgenstein, *Lectures and Conversations on Aesthetics, Psychology and Religious Belief*, ed. Cyril Barrett (Oxford: Blackwell, 1966)

Religious belief as basic

Alvin Plantinga, *Warranted Christian Belief* (New York: Oxford University Press, 2000)

James on belief

Graham Bird, *William James* (London: Routledge and Kegan Paul, 1986)

Richard M. Gale, *The Philosophy of William James: An Introduction* (Cambridge: Cambridge University Press, 2005)

William James, *The Will to Believe and Other Essays in Popular Philosophy* (New York: Longmans Green, 1897)

Chapter 6

Knowledge, truth and scientific progress

A. F. Chalmers, *What Is This Thing Called Science?*, 2nd edn. (Milton Keynes: Open University Press, 1982)

Bas van Fraassen, *The Scientific Image* (Oxford: Clarendon Press, 1982)

Moral agnosticism and moral scepticism

Clement Dore, *Moral Scepticism* (Basingstoke: Macmillan, 1991)

Colin Wilson, *The Outsider* (London: Victor Gollancz, 1956)

Pascal's Wager

J. L. Mackie, *The Miracle of Theism* (Oxford: Clarendon Press, 1982)

William G. Lycan and George N. Schlesinger, 'You Bet Your Life: Pascal's Wager Defended', in *Reason and Responsibility*, ed. Joel Feinberg (Belmont, CA: Wadsworth, 1989)

Agnosticism and religious commitment

Samantha Corte, 'Following God without Belief: Moral Objections to Agnostic Religious Commitment', *Philosophy Compass*, 3 (2008), 381–96

John Lemos, 'An Agnostic Defence of Obligatory Prayer', *Sophia*, 37 (1998), 70–87

Chapter 7
Uncertainty and creativity

Immanuel Wallerstein, 'Uncertainty and Creativity', *American Behavioural Scientist*, 42 (1998), 320–2

Game theory

William Poundstone, *Prisoner's Dilemma: John von Neumann, Game Theory, and the Puzzle of the Bomb* (Oxford: Oxford University Press, 1992)

Religion and science education

Thomas Dixon, *Science and Religion: A Very Short Introduction* (Oxford: Oxford University Press, 2008)

Michael J. Reiss, *Science Education for a Pluralist Society* (Buckingham: Open University Press, 1993)

Index

Page numbers in italics refer to illustrations.

Adam 1, 118
adaptation 14–15
Advertising Standards
    Agency 108–9
Agnostic Annual, The 2, *3*, 25
agnostic principle, the 26, 117
agnosticism
    arguments for 53, 57–76
    assumptions of 77–8
    as a creed 25–6
    definition of 8–9
    education and 111, 114–18
    evidential 13–17
    first use of term 2, 19–20
    about God's nature 10–13
    local versus global 10–13, 39
    knowledge and 4–5, 8–10, 97
    moral 100–1
    apparent negativity of 4
    origins of 10–11, 18–39
    in periodicals 22
    'poverty' of 2
    presumption of 53, 117
    (apparent) redundancy of 41–53
    religious life and 97–107
    scepticism and 13, 36–9
    scientific 13, 98–9, 101, 103
    as self-defeating 76

varieties of 9–17
    weak versus strong 9–10
ambiguous drawings 72
Anselm, St 10–11
antinomies of pure reason 28–9
Aquinas, St Thomas 11
argon, discovery of 55
Arnold, Matthew 98
artificial intelligence 59
Arundell, Isabel 21
ataraxia 36
atheism
    in relation to agnosticism 2, 4,
        8–9
    logical positivism and 81–3
    practical versus theoretical
        97–8
    presumption of 46–53
    temperament and 117
    and theism, arguments for
        57–76
'atheist buses' 108–110
Ayer, A.J. 79–81, *80*, 84

Baal 56
Bampton, John 23
Bampton Lectures 23–5, 27
Bédoyère, Quentin de la 2

belief
  basic 88–90
  degrees of 9, 14, 16–17, 96, 97, 117
  policies 93–6
Bible 6, 21, 55–6, 68
Big Bang hypothesis 14, 61
biology, *see* evolution; natural selection
blind sight 69
Bolt, Robert 76
Borel, Émile 113
Bradley, Stephen H. 67–9, 71–2
brain 70–1, 91
branding 1–2
British Humanist Association 108
Bultmann, Rudolf 85
burden of proof 43, 46, 53, 117; *see also* atheism, presumption of

Camus, Albert 100–1
categorical versus hypothetical imperative 30
causal necessity 33–4
chemistry 98–9
Christianity 13, 85, 108
Clifford, William Kingdom 91–4, *92*, 117
Clough, Arthur Hugh 98
cogito ergo sum 88
Cold War, the 113
conditioning 64–5
conscience 44, 63–7
consciousness 57, 59–60
creationism 116
creativity 111–14

Darwin, Charles 6, 19
Dawkins, Richard 2, 5, 6–7, 16–17, 42–3, 46, 53, 57, *110*
Descartes, René 87–8, 91
design, arguments from 34–5, 57–63, 74, 116
Dickens, Charles 114–15

dragon, the invisible 40–6, 51; *see also* teapot, the celestial

economics 6, 114–15
education 114–16
Elijah 56
emotion 83–4, 93–4, 96, 101, 102–7, 117
empiricism 26–7; *see also* logical empiricism
ethics of belief 91–6
evidential agnosticism 13–17
evolution 57–60, 116
extra-terrestrial life 5–6, 10

faith 15, 88–90, 91–6
faith schools 115–16
falsifiability 80
fiction 84, 86, 105–7
fine-tuning 60–3
free will 75, 87
Freudian theory 80
frivolous questions 86–7
fundamental constants 61–3

Galbraith, J.K. 6
game theory 113–14
Gladstone, W.E. 19
gnostics 21, 36
God,
  absence of 73–6
  conceptions of 11, 38, 51–2
  as creator 14, 44, 52
  existence of 8–9, 29–30, 35, 38, 86, 102–3
  experience and 29
  explanatory role of 52–3
  moral conscience and 63–7
  morality and 30, 52
  presence of 67–73
  reason and 29–30
  and suffering 73–6
  properties of 10–13
  see also theism
'God Helmet', the 70–1

Hampton, Christopher 100
history, teaching of 115
Horrocks, Jeremiah 54–5
Hume, David 30–5, *32*, 80
Hume's Fork 31–3, 34
Hutton, Richard 21, 22, 25
Huxley, Thomas Henry 18–23, *20*, 24–6, 30, 34, 36
hyperactive agency-detecting device 71, 91

imagery 85, 87, 106
intelligence 57–60

James, William 91–6, *95*, 102–4, 118
Jesus Christ 21, 106

Kant, Immanuel 27–31, *28*, 34, 35, 36
Kenny, Sir Anthony 51
Kepler, Johannes 54
knowledge 4, 5, 10, 27–8, 33, 97
Knowles, James 18–19
Korsakov's syndrome 112

laws of nature 60–3
life
   after death 45–6
   probability of 60–3
   purpose of 44, 74–5
logical positivism 34, 79–84
love 52, 74

Maimonides, Moses 11
make-believe 106, 118
Mansel, Henry Longueville 23–5, *24*, 27, 30
meaningfulness 79–85
Mendeleev, Dimitri 98
Metaphysical Society, The 19, 22
metaphysics 6, 79–80
mind, *see* consciousness;
   intelligence

Molière (Jean-Baptiste Poquelin) 100
moral agnosticism 100–1
moral conscience 63–7, 75
moral knowledge 52–3
moral truths 66–7
multiverse hypothesis 62–3

natural selection 7, 15, 19, 57–60, 65–6, 90, 116
naturalism 57
New Testament 68
Neumann, John von 113–14
Newman, John Henry 63–6, 73–4
Nineteenth Century, The 18
non-realism 86–7
noumenal versus phenomenal world 29

objectivity 66–7
Old Testament 55–6
Orwell, George 109
Oxford English Dictionary 21, 26

PAP (Permanent Agnosticism in Principle) 16
pain 66–7
Pascal's Wager 102–3, 104
Paul, St 21, 26
perception 69–70, 72, 89–90
Persinger, Michael 70
phlogiston 99
physics 99; *see also* laws of nature
Popper, Karl 80
'practical' *versus* 'theoretical' 97–8
prayer 13, 97, 104
prisoner's dilemma, the 113
Pritchard, Charles 18
probability 14, 16–17, 42–3, 49–53, 58, 61–3, 76, 111, 117, 118
projection 66–7
proof 7, 30, 37, 38, 42
Pyrrho 35–6
Pyrrhonian scepticism 13, 36–9

Ramsay, Sir William 55
randomness 57
rationalism 27–8
rationality 117
Rayleigh, Lord 55
realisation, variability of 59
regulative truth 24
relativism 118
religious experience 67–73, 89–91
religious language 10, 81, 83–7
religious non-realism 86–7
risk assessment 45–6
Robinson, Bishop John 85
Russell, Bertrand 41–3, 45

Sacks, Oliver 112
Sagan, Carl 40–1
scepticism 13, 35–9, 47–8, 90–1
Schlick, Moritz 78–9
scientific agnosticism 13,
    99–100, 103
scientific progress 98–9
self-deception 97–8
Sextus Empiricus *12*, 36–9
Spectator, The 21, 22
Spencer, Herbert 18, 25, 30, 36
Stanley, Dean Arthur 19
Stanley, Lady Augusta 19
Steady State hypothesis 13–14
Stephen, Leslie 18, 22–3
suffering, problem of 73–5
superfluity, problem of 74–5

TAP (Temporary Agnosticism in
    Practice) 16
teapot, the celestial 41–6, *43*, 51

Tennyson, Alfred Lord 18
theism
    arguments for 57–76
    in relation to agnosticism 2, 4,
        8–9
    logical positivism and 81–3
    predisposition towards 15, 71, 117
    as scientific hypothesis 15,
        17, 44–5, 51–3, 61–3, 81–3,
        104–5, 117
    see also faith; God
theological statements, meaning
    of 81–7
theory-ladenness of
    observation 71–2
Tillich, Paul 85
time 29, 38, 70
truth 77–8

ultimate reality 85
uncertainty 111–116, 118

Venus, transit of 54–5, 56
verifiability, principle of
    79–83
Vienna Circle 78–9

Wace, Henry 25
Watts, Charles 25
Williamson, Hugh Ross 2
Wittgenstein, Ludwig 84
Woolf, Virginia 18

'Young Earth' creationism 116

zombies 59–60

LOGIC
A Very Short Introduction
Graham Priest

Logic is often perceived as an esoteric subject, having little to do with the rest of philosophy, and even less to do with real life. In this lively and accessible introduction, Graham Priest shows how wrong this conception is. He explores the philosophical roots of the subject, explaining how modern formal logic deals with issues ranging from the existence of God and the reality of time to paradoxes of self-reference, change, and probability. Along the way, the book explains the basic ideas of formal logic in simple, non-technical terms, as well as the philosophical pressures to which these have responded. This is a book for anyone who has ever been puzzled by a piece of reasoning.

> 'a delightful and engaging introduction to the basic concepts of logic. Whilst not shirking the problems, Priest always manages to keep his discussion accessible and instructive.'
>
> **Adrian Moore, St Hugh's College, Oxford**

> 'an excellent way to whet the appetite for logic. . . . Even if you read no other book on modern logic but this one, you will come away with a deeper and broader grasp of the *raison d'être* for logic.'
>
> **Chris Mortensen, University of Adelaide**

www.oup.co.uk/isbn/0-19-289320-3

THEOLOGY
A Very Short Introduction
David F. Ford

This Very Short Introduction provides both believers
and non-believers with a balanced survey of the central
questions of contemporary theology. David Ford's inter-
rogative approach draws the reader into considering the
principles underlying religious belief, including the central-
ity of salvation to most major religions, the concept of
God in ancient, modern, and post-modern contexts, the
challenge posed to theology by prayer and worship, and
the issue of sin and evil. He also probes the nature of
experience, knowledge, and wisdom in theology, and
discusses what is involved in interpreting theological
texts today.

> 'David Ford tempts his readers into the huge resources of
> theology with an attractive mix of simple questions and
> profound reflection. With its vivid untechnical language it
> succeeds brilliantly in its task of introduction.'
> **Stephen Sykes, University of Durham**

> 'a fine book, imaginatively conceived and gracefully writ-
> ten. It carries the reader along with it, enlarging horizons
> while acknowledging problems and providing practical
> guidance along the way.'
> **Maurice Wiles, University of Oxford**

www.oup.co.uk/vsi/theology